The Choice Is Yours

A TEENAGER'S GUIDE TO SELF-DISCOVERY, RELATIONSHIPS, VALUES, AND SPIRITUAL GROWTH

Bonnie M. Parsley

Foreword by
M. Scott Peck, M.D.

A FIRESIDE BOOK
Published by Simon & Schuster
New York   London   Toronto   Sydney   Tokyo   Singapore

F FIRESIDE

Rockefeller Center
1230 Avenue of the Americas
New York, New York, 10020

Designed by Irving Perkins Associates
Manufactured in the United States of America

10 9 8 7 6 5 4

Library of Congress Cataloging-in-Publication Data

Parsley, Bonnie M.
    The choice is yours : a teenager's guide to self-discovery,
relationships, values, and spiritual growth / Bonnie M.
Parsley ; foreword by M. Scott Peck.
        p.   cm.
    "A Fireside book."
    Includes bibliographical references.
    Summary: Discusses the proper decisions that can lead
to a healthy and fulfilling life, examining such areas as
school, parents, dating, and drugs.
    1. Teenagers—Conduct of life. 2. Teenagers—
Religious life. [1. Conduct of life.] I. Title.
BJ1661.P275 1992
170'.835—dc20   92-3697
                                                        CIP
                                                         AC

ISBN: 0-671-75046-1

To my husband, Don, for his love, encouragement, and support

Contents

Contents

Foreword

by M. Scott Peck, M.D.

For years many people have asked me if I had ever thought about writing a version of *The Road Less Traveled* for teenagers. Frankly, ten years ago I would have considered such a book unrealistic. How could a teenager make the choice to be as mature as the book would recommend? And what would give an author the right to suggest that the teenager try to be even more mature, sometimes, than his or her own parents?

But over the past ten years I have received a lot of letters from healthy teenagers and have had the opportunity to work with many such young people in community-building workshops. These experiences have shown me that it is indeed possible for many teenagers to consciously choose a path of spiritual growth. And when it happens, it can be glorious.

As a result I have changed my mind, and when people have approached me with the idea of a book for teenagers, I always reply, "You do it." Now, someone has finally done it—and done it well.

The title of Bonnie Parsley's book is an accurate one: *The Choice Is Yours*. It is a very smart choice, but I do not mean to imply that it is an easy one. Putting into practice the decision to choose a path of spiritual growth is not something you can do in a week. In fact, you will be doing it for the rest of your life. And you will be doing it one day at a time. Furthermore, there is no way you can do it perfectly. You will fall short again and again and again. That's all right. It's to be expected. You may feel bad when you fall short, but don't feel too bad. You are even entitled to feel sorry for yourself on this difficult lifelong journey of growing up (but not more than five minutes twice a day). The point is to simply stay with the choice.

The choice is possible, and it is yours. I hope you will make it.

Introduction

Who are you? If you react as most people do to that question, you will tell me your name. But I'm not satisfied with just your name, so I repeat, "Who are you . . . I mean who are you, really?" Now you may begin to describe yourself. I'm a boy—a girl . . . I'm blond or redheaded . . . tall or plump . . . black or white . . . Christian or Jewish. After you've finished labeling yourself and describing yourself, I still am not satisfied, for I know there is more to you than your body and the labels you've given yourself.

My purpose in writing this book is to help you awaken to yourself—to realize that within you lies the real you. Why do I want to do this? Because I remember how difficult it was to be a teenager. Also, as a teacher, I have watched young people in my classes grappling with the problems of growing up. As the mother of four daughters, I've lived the hurts and struggles with each of them, and seen distress and suffering in the lives of their friends. The years between twelve and twenty are tough. This time of a young person's life can be challenging, perplexing, worrisome, wonderful, and terrible, and all this can be fatiguing. It can also be disturbing and disastrous. But it doesn't have to be.

If someone were to offer you a key to a great treasure, would you take it? The great treasure is you, and by discovering yourself now, you can live your adolescent years with confidence, understanding, and a sense of well-being. You have a right to self-discovery, but you must choose to take the key and unlock the treasure yourself.

It takes a lifetime of struggle and futility for many of us to realize what life is all about. If we could discover ourselves at the beginning, when we're just starting out, how much better our lives might be. I don't ask you to believe me. I only ask you to be open. A person who already has his mind made up about life cannot be open. Openness is the spirit of willingness to look at—to consider—something that may be new or different from things you've heard before. Be open but believe nothing until you see the truth of it with your own heart. When you begin to see the truth of something deep within your being, it becomes more than belief. It becomes real, something known and not just believed. Truth, like a rose unfolding its petals, blossoms within your heart when you allow yourself the freedom to be open.

In many ways teenagers today are in crisis. Though parents have done a sufficient job supplying their physical needs, and educators have struggled to train their minds, it hasn't been enough. Teens have more issues to face currently than ever before. They need more than food, shelter, clothing, and education to deal with the world in which they live today. There is another side to the individual that must not be ignored. This is his spiritual side. The teen who has in his heart the spiritual keys that lead to wisdom will be able to meet the challenges of the changing world and will not only survive his teenage years but live them joyfully.

Be happy, my friend,
For you do have a choice,
You can sit and complain
Or stand and rejoice.
You can waste your life
With judgment and blame,
Or learn to forgive
And understand we're the same.

For all of us feel fear
And everyone knows pain,
Products of experience,
No one's to blame.
So let go of your past,
Your hurts and your fears,
Cherish each moment
And love life while you're here.

CHAPTER I

Loving Yourself

Many people cringe when they hear someone talk of self-love. They immediately picture an egotist—a totally self-absorbed person who thinks only of his own welfare. But the selfishness that drives egotism is totally contrary to the motivation of self-love. Many of us misunderstand what loving yourself is all about because we misunderstand the nature of love.

Love has become so many things and the term is so general that we use the word for just about anything. We can love other people and we can love ourselves, but we cannot love a thing. We associate love with a feeling, and the problem is that, although love may generate a feeling, it is not the feeling. Love is the action that comes before the feeling.

I like to think of love as the act of helping oneself or another person to grow spiritually. By spirituality we can mean many things. Almost every religion equates spirit with God or some transforming greater force. In Western civilization the Christian experience has gained the largest following. In other parts of the world Buddhism, Hinduism, Judaism, and other religions are devoutly followed. Some people who profess no particular religion demonstrate by their character and the way they live their lives that they are deeply spiritual beings. No matter how we choose to define spirituality, there is one

15

common thread: our spirituality reminds us of a dimension that is greater than our physical selves and our material needs.

It remains for each one of us to determine how our own personal form of spirituality can guide us through life. As we grow spiritually, we begin to awaken to our true selves, to have confidence in who we really are. We begin to see things we could not see before. Our life's purpose reveals itself to us and our potential becomes unlimited. All things suddenly seem possible.

By loving ourselves we are showing a willingness to feed, or care for, our own spiritual growth. With this in mind we can understand that loving the self has nothing to do with egotism. The egotist is really suffering from spiritual need. The individual who has learned to love himself has become a nurturer, a caretaker for his own well-being.

Loving ourselves does not come easy. In fact, it can be very hard work. After all, we first have to get by all the taboos against loving ourselves.

Traditional religion doesn't encourage a person to love himself. Rather the opposite is true. Much religion tells us that we are born in sin and doomed to spend eternity in Hell unless we repent of our sins. Notice, we are not encouraged to understand our sins but to hate ourselves for having them. We are told that the only way to reach salvation is by believing something that we are told is true. We are discouraged from questioning and told we must accept on faith. The idea of loving ourselves the way we are is considered depraved—wrong.

Many of our parents don't encourage us to love ourselves because that has never been part of a parent's job description. Parents are supposed to make us behave properly and be polite. Some of the most vivid words from my childhood are my mother saying, "Bonnie, you should be ashamed of yourself!" I don't remember, however, her saying I should feel proud of myself or good about myself even when I'd accomplished something special. It wasn't that she was a bad parent. She was just raising me in the traditional way—the same way she was raised. Children were expected to do well, and only bad behavior got attention. Nevertheless, we must realize that our parents are doing the best they know how. Their skill (or lack thereof) for parenting came from their parents, whose skill in turn came from their parents, extending back to the beginning of time. Parents often can't teach their children to love themselves because *they* have never been taught that.

Teachers aren't concerned with us loving ourselves. They are too busy pointing out our errors and keeping order in the classroom. They are busy teaching us, controlling us, and judging us. Some, out of frustration, resort to ridicule, threats, anger, and punishment to accomplish these things. Of course, there are people out there—parents and teachers—who help us believe in ourselves and give us the recognition we crave. When we find them, we never forget them. I had a drama teacher in high school who was like that. Mr. Scales was tough. He demanded our best effort; he was always there to help us, encourage us, and support us, and we knew he cared. I had taken drama because I thought it would be an easy A, but I ended up working harder in that class than in any other. I participated in all the plays that year, attending rehearsals two or three hours every school night, and I took part in play festivals and contests on weekends. Going into that class, I never had any

idea that I would become so involved, but Mr. Scales
ignited my creativity, and his caring made me care. At
the end of the year I won an award for Best Thespian of
the Year. I never would have done it without Mr. Scales.

Unfortunately many young people never find that
special person who helps them to discover themselves.
More than a few teens feel unloved and unlovable. From
the time they were small children, they have taken all
the bad things that happened personally. They feel at
fault when Mom gets angry and yells. They feel guilty if
Mom and Dad get divorced. The mere expression of
emotion is discouraged or forbidden by many parents.
"Don't cry . . . don't be angry . . . be quiet and sit down!"
They feel shame for expressing their feelings, so they
close down to protect themselves. They decide they are
unloved and unlovable, and without realizing it, they set
out to prove it.

Beginning in about fifth or sixth grade kids group
together, and anyone who is at all different may be ex-
cluded. Since each one of us is unique, if others look
closely enough they can come up with something about
us they don't like. At one time or another, most of us
will experience rejection from our peers, and this rejection can be pure devastation to a young person. What is
really devastating, however, is what that adolescent may
do with the rejection he experiences. If he uses it to
convince himself further that he is unloved and unlovable, it is tragic. Rejection hurts, it causes pain and con-
fusion, but we don't have to let it destroy us. Remember,
people don't treat you unlovingly because you are unlovable but because they lack love within themselves.

We need to love ourselves, for until we do, there can
be no spiritual growth. Loving yourself and deeply val-

uing yourself gives you the courage to become a unique, independent person and totally you. Knowing that you are a valuable person is essential to your well-being. It is necessary for self-discipline. If you consider yourself valuable, you will take care of yourself, and you will forgive your mistakes. If you love yourself, you'll be kind with yourself, and you won't expect perfection.

Once, when one of my daughters was in her early teens, she was at home alone while I had gone for a walk. As I rounded a corner and started uphill toward home, I saw her racing toward me, sock-footed and with an expression of pure misery on her face.

"I just lost a thousand dollars!" she howled.

"What happened," I asked, noting the tears in her eyes.

"B-100 Radio called and asked if I knew their slogan. I couldn't think," she blurted between sobs. "I know it . . . I listen to it all the time. It's . . ." and she repeated the slogan word for word. Suddenly her hurt was replaced with anger at herself. "I'm so stupid!" she erupted. "I hate myself. I can't do anything right."

It seemed as though I was listening to my own voice from the past. I had spent many years hating myself for not being perfect. I had been my own worst critic, constantly replaying my conversations and actions and labeling myself unmercifully. Fortunately, I learned that the only thing self-criticism brings is unhappiness.

"You had a momentary lapse of memory," I told her. "That happens to everyone. It doesn't mean you're stupid."

"But it was a thousand dollars!"

"I know you feel bad about not winning the money. I would feel bad, too, but you can't hate yourself for that."

Her eyes squeezed tighter. "I can't believe it. One chance in a million they'd call and I miss it."

I understood the agony she was feeling. "You have to forgive yourself," I told her. "Be kind to yourself and give yourself permission to fail once in a while." I wished someone had told me that when I was her age. It took me many long years to learn this lesson.

How do we get the idea that we are not worthy of being loved just as we are? Why do we feel we must do everything perfectly before we can give love to ourselves? We can never receive love from ourselves or anyone else until we are ready to acknowledge our own value. We must make a conscious choice to love ourselves regardless of outside circumstances. This is unconditional love, the kind of love that is given without reservation. Keep in mind that love is a willingness to help ourselves awaken spiritually. Loving yourself is not the same thing as being conceited. In fact, inherent in conceit or vanity is a large amount of pride. In order to truly love ourselves, pride is one of the things that must be dropped. Can we allow ourselves to be less than perfect if pride rules our lives?

Loving yourself involves caring about yourself and never doing anything that you know would be harmful to either your body, your mind, or your spirit. It's taking time to go inside—to get in touch with your spiritual nature. Getting very quiet, emptying your mind of all thought, allows the spirit within you to be revealed, to be known. Some call this the Christ spirit or God within. When we become very quiet, it's like listening to God. It's like letting go of yourself for a while in order to experience something larger than you.

A final reason why we need to love ourselves is that we

cannot love others until we love ourselves first. If you hate someone, try accepting your feelings about that person. Then try to understand where those feelings come from. Does the person make you feel bad about yourself? If you truly loved yourself, could anyone make you feel bad about you? Perhaps the person makes you angry because they're rude and obnoxious. By learning not to judge yourself so harshly and understanding your own faults, you will be better able to understand why others do some of the things they do. By learning to forgive your own mistakes, you will be able to forgive others theirs.

So the key is to genuinely love yourself. Then when someone tries to make you feel bad about yourself, they will not succeed, and therefore you will not hate them. Loving yourself frees you to understand why others act the way they do, and this enables you to have compassion for them.

FINDING THE LOVE YOU NEED

If no one has ever told you that you are special and are loved, then how can you love yourself? There is only one way. You must stop looking for other people to convince you that you are lovable. Go inside yourself for the love you need, for that is where love comes from. It comes from a willingness in our heart to love—to reach out to ourselves—for the purpose of finding a deeper consciousness or awareness. You have to become your own champion, best friend, or parent, however you want to imagine it. You have to give yourself what no one else has given you—compassion, understanding, caring, and encouragement.

Loving yourself is accepting yourself totally. What good does it do to moan over things you can't change? You can work to be the very best "you" possible, but there are basic things you can't change. You can't change your height, your body type, your race, or the family into which you were born. Once you accept yourself, even your imperfections, and feel deep down that you are okay, then and only then can you begin progress down the path of spiritual awareness. Also remember that you are much more than your body—a temporary body that will eventually wear out. The important part of you—the spiritual part—will be with you always. Make sure that part is well cared for, accept the rest, and make the most of it.

ACCEPTING YOUR FEELINGS

A very important part of accepting yourself totally is accepting your feelings, including the negative ones. Never resist feeling something, whether it's sadness, fear, anger, or whatever. Feel it and accept it totally. Only through accepting the feeling and understanding where it came from can we finally let go of our negative responses, such as fear and anger, and be free again. When you stop resisting your feelings—denying them, burying them, and hating yourself for them—and start understanding them, then it will be possible to love yourself.

Repressing and denying our feelings can make us ill. Our immune system doesn't work well under stress, and repressing something is very stressful. Have you ever had something unpleasant happen and you just wanted to forget it? The more you tried to forget it, the more it plagued your mind. It's like when your boyfriend or girlfriend breaks up with you and you want to push it out of your thoughts. Your mind, however, won't let it go, and you find that's all you can think of. The more you dwell on it, the harder you work to push it out of your mind. Thus begins an exhausting, never-ending circle. This circle of trying to forget, or deny, and then remembering again is very hard work. When you're throwing all your energy into this one activity, other things suffer—work, school, and your mental and physical health.

Feelings can cause great hurt, and it's not surprising that we'd want to escape from the pain. So we try running away from our feelings by repressing them. Running away never works, however, because you end up taking you along. Feelings must be confronted and understood.

If you are feeling angry, ask yourself, "Where does this anger come from? Why do I feel this way?" Get past the action or words that make you angry and find the underlying cause. The obvious cause is rarely the root cause. This is hidden within you and will take some self-examination to understand.

If you will make the effort, you will find that, in one way or another, your ego has been threatened. Think of your ego as a beautiful, fragile work of art that you have spent years creating. You've put everything you have into this masterpiece: your time, your money, your hopes and dreams—everything. Now someone comes along and threatens to punch a hole in it. You rush in to defend it; your heart races and your palms sweat. You will do anything it takes to protect your art—your ego.

Angie's friend Jill says she'll call her on Saturday.

Saturday comes and goes, and Jill never calls. Angie feels angry. Maybe Jill doesn't want to be her friend anymore. This means that she will have to eat lunch alone on Monday, and she doesn't want to eat alone. People might laugh at her if she has to eat alone. If Angie would think about it for a while and realize that her anger is coming from her fear that she may be alone, rather than the fact that her friend didn't call, she could face that fear and tell herself that, whether or not she ate alone, she would still be the same person. She would still be Angie, and being alone wouldn't change that. Then she might be able to realize that being alone for a while isn't the end of the world. Now she can let go of her anger toward Jill, and the girls will be less likely to get into a fight the next time they are together.

When we finally understand that our anger comes from the hurt buried inside us, or perhaps from the fear of being alone, the fear of being hurt, or the fear of being out of control, then we've found the source of our anger. When we recognize that source, a strange thing happens. Our anger suddenly begins to melt away, and we are soon free of its terrible hold on us.

Resisting our feelings, rather than being open to them and admitting them, keeps the feelings locked inside. Only through recognizing them can they be felt, understood, and then released.

UNDERSTANDING OTHER PEOPLE'S ANGER

People's need to hurt others often comes from the fact that they are so deeply hurt themselves that the only way they can feel good is to hurt someone else the way they've been hurt. If a teen experiences being shamed at home, he may repress a lot of anger and resentment. He buries this anger and resentment in his subconscious, the part of his mind of which he is unaware. He does this because he has learned that feelings such as anger, hate, and fear are not acceptable. Later these buried feelings come exploding out of him. When these negative emotions come out, they are rarely directed at the person who shamed him in the first place. They get dumped on the kids at school or his teachers, and sometimes they get dumped on himself. We must try to remember that when someone strikes out at us in anger, their outburst may have nothing to do with us. Their anger may be coming from their repressed feelings or, in many cases, from their fears. Mary gets home late from a date with a new boyfriend. "Where have you been?" her father yells, his face becoming red and his eyes full of fury. "When I say eleven o'clock, I mean eleven o'clock!"

"We were only talking and lost track of the time," Mary tries to explain.

"You're irresponsible. I can't trust you," he says bitterly. "You're grounded for two weeks," and he stomps out of the room.

Mary becomes angry with her father. "I hate him," she complains to her girlfriend. "He never listens to me. He's impossibly strict and I can't wait until I move out!"

Instead of becoming resentful, Mary could choose to respond differently to her father's anger. She could try to understand where it is coming from. If she can see beyond her father's temper and beyond his striking words, and recognize that it was his fear and concern for her that set him off, she will be able to release her own anger. This is not the natural thing to do. Our primitive instinct tells us, when confronted with anger, to respond with anger. We can move beyond that instinct, however, and force ourselves to a more intelligent way of dealing with other people's anger. Through understanding we can overcome the tendency to fight back. This willingness to understand, rather than fight, is a sign that we are progressing spiritually.

THE LAW OF ALLOWANCE

We need to allow whatever is in our life to be there. Resisting is wasted energy. When we allow it, we can begin to understand it. If Lindy has been verbally abused by her mother, she may want to deny that her mother is doing this. She may be angry at her or even feel she hates her, but deep down she may be saying, *I must deserve this or my mother wouldn't do this to me.* Instead of blaming herself or her mother, Lindy could simply admit what is happening. *Mom is angry with me.* Lindy should resist drawing conclusions: *Mom doesn't love me— I'm a bad kid.* Now, after allowing the verbal abuse into her life, without any judgments, Lindy can begin to understand it. *Why does my mother say these hurtful things to me? What experience in her past taught her to do this? Is she motivated by frustration or exhaustion? What feelings are behind her words?* Lindy must see that she is the target of her mother's abuse, not the cause. No one can be the cause of another person's abuse. The cause is within the abuser's past unresolved experiences or in his or her fears. In many cases, an abusive parent was himself abused as a child. If he never worked through his own feelings about the abuse, it is likely that he will repeat the pattern. As a child he never had any control. Now, as an adult, he demands total control.

Being willing to experience what is actually happening, whether it's that your mom is verbally abusing you, or your father is an alcoholic, or your friend is using you, lets you dispel—get rid of—your illusions. Now you can see things as they really are. You are no longer fooling yourself. This can be painful, but it is the first step in setting yourself free.

Experiencing the truth requires courage and determination. Being willing to see things the way they are and accepting them directs us toward the light of reality. Resisting things by wishing they were different, hoping they will change, or rationalizing their appearance as something else entirely only creates illusion in our minds.

In order to see things the way they are, we must be willing to drop our resistance to pain, because in seeing the truth we may experience great pain or fear. Teenagers will find out that their parents, friends, and other people they love are not perfect. In fact, some of them may discover the harsh reality that they have been abused or used. Admitting this is painful. Only by seeing these things and admitting them, however, and going through the pain and fear that this knowledge brings will we awaken to reality.

At this point it becomes possible to love yourself and others unconditionally. You now have the awareness that allows you to begin a process of change. When you can admit what is happening, you can start to resolve your problems. In the case of child abuse, teenagers will probably need outside help. They can talk to a school counselor, their minister, or any understanding adult whom they feel can be confided in. The main thing is to find help. Abuse should never be allowed to continue. That would be unloving. If we love someone who is being abusive, we must help start the healing process; otherwise we and the abuser will suffer spiritually.

So acknowledge whatever is in your life. Accept it, feel it, understand it, and resolve it. If you will do all this, the pain it has caused you will finally dissolve, and a healing of your spirit will occur.

LETTING GO OF THE NEED FOR APPROVAL

Everyone has had experiences of being treated harshly or cruelly. This happens especially frequently when we are growing up because kids at school can be very cruel. However, we make a mistake when we use these unfortunate experiences to convince ourselves that we are worthless and unloved, and that therefore something must be wrong with us. Then we start feeling bad about ourselves, wishing we were different, more popular, prettier, more athletic, smarter. We hunger for attention and recognition, and find that many times "things" get us this attention—new clothes, toys, and, later, cars and the right person by our side. We get satisfaction from this attention, and this is the beginning of our desire for more things.

Something else that gets us the attention and recognition that we need is doing what other people want us to do. We strive to get straight A's, not for our own education and knowledge, but for Mom and Dad's approval. We work hard on our merit badges in Scouts, we take music lessons, clean the house, walk the dog—not out of love for our parents or ourselves, but for the recognition we get for it. Whenever our motivation is to gain recognition or to meet someone else's expectations, we will be left with a sense of emptiness. Rather than looking inward for our own expectations, we continue to look outside of ourselves; we look to others for approval and lose touch with what we want.

So we learn to hide who we are behind our accomplishments and our possessions. After many years of amassing and achieving we still feel that something's missing. We have no sense of satisfaction. We realize that all of these things haven't gotten us the love we wanted so badly. We realize that everything has been futile. When we reach the point of futility, we feel very low indeed.

Do we have to reach the point of futility before we realize that we can't look outside ourselves for the love we need? Perhaps you can decide now, in the beginning of your life, to choose the path of love. After all, that's really all it is—a choice. If we choose the path of love, we must first love ourselves, accept ourselves exactly the way we are. When we can do this, we will, for the first time in our lives, be genuine. At this time, surprisingly enough, when we are no longer looking for love from outside of us, others will find us more lovable. Just as people are attracted to a genuine artifact, people are attracted to someone who is real.

WHAT LOVE IS NOT

Loving yourself does not mean always having your own way or always being in control. It also doesn't mean giving in to your desires. Desire and the need for control come from the ego. Your ego is something you've created. It's the self that you think you are, but it's not the real you. The real you is spirit, and when you truly love yourself, you know instinctively that always getting your way is bad for you. You know, too, that always giving in to your desires is hurtful. The child who always gets his way becomes spoiled, bad-tempered, and hard to get along with. The teen who has everything his heart desires finds that it's never enough. He never feels satisfied. He keeps trying to fill his cup of desire, but he finds that the cup has no bottom and is impossible to fill.

There is only one thing that we should allow as our motivation and that is love. We do things for our parents because we care for them, we value their opinions, we love them. We do things for others for the same reason. When we learn to love ourselves enough, we will be able to give up our craving for recognition. Recognition can be great, but if we let it become our motivation, we will never be satisfied.

So love yourself! You don't have to be perfect. You don't have to get straight A's or be captain of the football team. You just need to surrender to being yourself. If you truly love yourself you won't do a single thing that would harm you. You won't call yourself stupid or think a single thought that would corrupt you. You won't do things for the wrong reasons. You will, however, recognize the uniqueness of you. You will find joy in just being yourself without the need for a mask. And, finally, you will be able to love others as you love yourself.

CHAPTER II

Friendships, Dating, and Falling in Love

Many lasting friendships are formed during our teenage years. We may even meet that special someone who becomes our lifetime partner. But sometimes a teen will enter into a relationship with another person for the wrong reasons, perhaps because of pressures from the outside or because of insecurities of his own. These friendships can be devastating. When our friendships aren't going well we can get depressed, physically ill, or have trouble eating and sleeping. It's important that we understand our need for friends, and how our relationships can be healthy or unhealthy, according to how we see them.

THE NEED TO BELONG

It's natural for teenagers to want to be part of a group. The need to belong can be very strong in all of us, no matter what our age. Do you remember, as a child, ever being separated from your parents? The thought of being alone can be terrifying. We begin to see ourselves as part of a group from an early age. First we identify with our family and become dependent on our parents and siblings for security and stability. If one member of the family dies or leaves (as in divorce), it is traumatic and upsetting. Our view of ourselves—the picture in our mind that tells us who we are—has been altered. We feel troubled by the change.

When we start school we become a kid in Miss Bell's class or Mrs. Jamison's class. Being an accepted member of a certain class makes us feel secure. Now we can leave our family for a few hours every day to become part of another group at school. By the time we reach sixth grade, friendships have become one of the most important things in our lives. If we have a group of friends, or even just one good friend, and if we are getting along well with them, our lives are generally happy (assuming things are okay at home). When these friends are fighting with us, however, our whole world seems dark, sad, and forbidding.

Then we become teenagers, and it becomes more important than ever to have friends. We become more selective and we must have the "right" friends. Rejection at this age can be like a saw blade running through our middle. If we can let go of this desperate need to belong—to be part of a group—we can save ourselves a great deal of pain and unhappiness. When we make belonging a need, we cannot feel free to be ourselves. We try to be what we think the others in the group want us to be. We create a facade—a false face—because we are afraid to be ourselves and risk being rejected by the new friends we've made. Jenny says Kara's dress is ugly and you agree, even though you like her dress. John says a certain rock group is excellent and you go along with him or say nothing, but you know you don't like them. It's not that we should get into an argument with someone every time we disagree, but we shouldn't let them think we feel one way when we don't.

When you cloak your real feelings and pretend to be something you're not, the other kids will soon find you out. You will be telling one person in the group one thing and changing it when talking to someone else. If you're always saying and doing things to please others, you are not being genuine. You are not being real, and the other kids will soon lose respect for you.

The key to having great friendships is our ability to strip ourselves of any masks we may have hidden behind and to let another person see us as we are. We must allow ourselves to be vulnerable—unguarded and completely open and honest. At the same time we must balance our honesty with common sense. Close friendships grow over a period of time through shared experiences as well as shared thoughts. Though we should be honest about our feelings for other people and not afraid to express our affection for them, we should temper our openness and honesty with prudence. We can take our time getting to know someone. We don't need to reveal everything about ourselves the first time we meet.

Sometimes we become impulsive about a new friendship. If we try to rush things too fast, we may actually scare the other person away. A good friendship is not made hastily. Thoughtful consideration is the attitude we need to use when it comes to finding friends. Always remember how drastically friendships can affect us during the teenage years. Being with the right people can sometimes make the difference between life and death when we are teenagers, so we should take our time and choose our friends wisely.

Recently one of my daughters was struggling with a decision to stay with her current group of friends or find other friends. "Jasmine tells me what to do, and if

I don't do what she wants, she gets mad and says she'll never speak to me again. Then she stomps off, taking the other girls with her," my daughter complained. "She makes me so angry, I don't know why I stay friends with her."

"Why do you?" I asked.

"Because if I drop her, I won't have anybody," she grumbled.

"Can't you find another group of friends?"

Her eyes filled with pain. "It's hard to get into another group."

"So . . . it's easier to stay in a group where you're miserable than work at getting accepted into another group?"

She looked at me hotly. "You just don't understand!"

"I understand it's not easy leaving the security of a group you're familiar with. I understand it's risky approaching other groups and trying to work your way in. I also understand that it's important to your happiness to surround yourself with friends who respect you and don't try to manipulate or control you."

"So you think I should drop them?"

"I'm not telling you what to do. You have to decide what's best for you. Continuing to give in to Jasmine isn't making you happy. You've got a problem, and you must decide the best way to solve it," I told her. After thinking it over, my daughter was able to come up with several different ways of dealing with her problem. She surprised herself when she found that there were more than two options—staying or leaving. She thought of siding with one of the other girls the next time Jasmine tried to manipulate one of them, thereby gaining an ally for her next confrontation. She thought of hanging around with another group for a few days to show she could get along without Jasmine. She also realized that she could confront Jasmine and tell her how she had to treat her if they were to remain friends. As she recognized the many choices that she had, she discovered her own confidence to handle the situation. The important thing was that she took charge of her own happiness and was willing to work at reestablishing a feeling of harmony in her life.

When we face the fact that not everyone is going to like us and know deep down that's okay; when we can accept rejection without feeling responsible for it; when we know deeply that we can be alone sometimes and we won't die—then we can let go of the need to belong. Belonging to a group shouldn't be a need. It should be a choice we make.

DEEPENING OUR FRIENDSHIPS

Friendship begins with kindness, an important ingredient of any relationship no matter how long we've known the person. Little acts of kindness show someone we really care about them. We can take them a book if they're sick or remember them on a special day. We can ask them how we can help if they are having difficulties.

Being kind is being tolerant. Our friends are going to do things that bother us. They're going to tease and be a pain in the neck at times, but we don't have to get mad. We don't have to react in anger and lash out with thoughtless words. We can be tolerant of them. Let them be themselves. As long as they aren't causing us some kind of permanent harm, can't we just let it go?

One reason we don't let it go is that we allow what our

friend says or does to hurt our feelings. If someone says to you that your nose is purple, you'd laugh; it wouldn't bother you because you know good and well that your nose is not purple. However, if someone says that you are dumb, have ugly hair, or are a jerk, you become angry. To the degree that we are not sure of ourselves and feel threatened by the statement, we will feel anger. The more unsure of ourselves we are, the more anger we will feel.

We must know who we are so well that we will not be hurt by things our friends might say. Instead of taking offense and becoming angry, we can look at ourselves. Instead of judging our friend as being mean and thoughtless, we can try some self-examination. Ask yourself, "Have I been unkind? Have I done something that has caused my friend to act this way?" If we look at ourselves rather than condemn our friend, we can grow from the experience. We may find out things about ourselves that we haven't wanted to admit. Being willing to look at our own flaws is the first step toward wholeness. If, on the other hand, we find that there is nothing we've done to cause the unkindness, we can try to understand why our friend is acting that way. By trying to understand another person's cruelty, we open the door to our compassion. When we see that our friend's remark has come from his own insecurities, fears, or prejudice, we will no longer feel hurt. We can tell our friend that we're sorry he feels a certain way, and let it go at that.

There are times, however, when we can't just let it go. When our friend is doing something that could hurt our relationship or harm himself or others, we need to speak up. Friendship should allow for confrontation. This means that we need to be able to face each other with the truth. Without the freedom to confront each other, our friendship is superficial. The relationship is shallow and will never be fulfilling.

Jason and Kip had been friends since sixth grade. The boys were opposites in many ways. Jason was quiet and laid back. Kip was boisterous and always on the move. Jason was very religious and Kip wasn't into church at all. Their different interests only seemed to strengthen their friendship. Their personalities complemented each other; because of their differences, each found his life expanded. Each admired the other, and they genuinely liked being together. Early in their friendship they recognized the fact that their differences could cause conflict, and so they vowed that they would never argue. They thought their vow would preserve their friendship forever. By the end of high school Jason had become a whiz with auto engines and Kip was into sports, but they still spent their spare time together and continued to be best friends. As the boys matured into young men, their childhood vow became a wedge that began to force them apart.

"I know Jason promised he'd get the engine fixed on your car," Kip explained to his girlfriend. "I don't understand what's the matter with him."

"You've got to talk to him," she said. "Ask him what the problem is."

"I have asked, several times. If I say any more it'll cause an argument, and ... well, you know about our vow."

"You and your stupid vow!" she exploded. Are you friends or aren't you? If your friendship can't survive a little conflict, it's meaningless."

At first Kip was irritated by his girlfriend's criticism, but after thinking about it he saw that she had a good point. We must be able to confront and criticize, in a loving way, for our friendships to be meaningful and close. When Kip realized this he went to Jason with the truth.

"You're getting me in a lot of hot water with my girl," Kip explained. "I talked her into letting you fix her car and promised her you'd have it done in a week, which was what you'd told me. Now it's been three weeks, it's still not done, and she's yelling at me."

Jason was surprised that Kip was so upset by the situation, but apologetic, explaining that he had been procrastinating for no particular reason. He got busy on the car and had it done before the day was out.

Generally our fear of confronting someone doesn't result in the terrible consequences that we may imagine, and we find that truthful communication releases anger and resentment, and leads to a more lasting and harmonious friendship.

If we don't feel free to express our feelings we cannot have a truly deep friendship. If our friend is doing or saying something that is dangerous or harmful to himself or another person, either physically or spiritually, we must speak up or we will lose respect for ourselves. Keeping quiet when we know we should speak out is unloving. Sometimes the most loving thing we can do is to confront our friend.

Deciding whether to confront a friend or to end a friendship is a decision that must be made with wisdom and understanding. Ultimately the decision must depend on what is best for you. If the relationship is not supportive and based on equality, respect, and honesty,

and there is no hope for making it that way, then perhaps it is time to end it. If, on the other hand, the
friendship usually has these ingredients but some slight
or misunderstanding has caused hurt, it would be wise
to clear up the problem with loving confrontation.

I wish I'd had the courage to confront friends when I
was a teenager. I was fortunate not to have friends who
got into dangerous situations, but there were times when
I got so upset by something a friend had done that I
ended the friendship. I wish I had confronted them and
tried to work it out, but my ego was too fragile at the
time. When our egos are fragile, they crack very easily,
and this is painful. Rather than endure the pain and risk
more pain by confrontation, I would run away and find
another friend. For me, it was easier to risk rejection
from a stranger than risk it with someone who had been
my friend.

In his book *The Friendship Factor,* Alan Loy McGinnis
writes that one way we can deepen our friendships is to
talk about our feelings. Our feelings are the guideposts
to our inner selves. Sharing our feelings with a friend
creates a kind of intimacy between us that draws us
closer. Sharing our feelings says that we trust our friend,
and it bonds us like nothing else can.

To have great friendships you don't have to be witty
or talk a lot, but you do need to know how to listen. If
you can really listen to another person and not be thinking about what you are going to say in response, people
will want to be with you. People who monopolize the
conversation soon find themselves with no one to talk to.
In his book, McGinnis lists five traits of a good listener.
If we would memorize these five traits and always practice them, our friendships would become deeper.

McGinnis says that good listeners listen with their eyes. Have you ever been talking to someone and they look away from you? They let their eyes wander all around the room as you speak. I had a friend in college who did this. It drove me crazy and, after putting up with it for a few weeks, I began to stop talking when he would look away. It wasn't long before he got the point. We don't like people to do this. It says they don't care what we have to say, that they really aren't interested. When we listen to someone, we respond to what they are saying with our eyes. We show encouragement, understanding, and compassion with our eyes, and we build intimacy.

McGinnis cautions us to be careful when giving advice to a friend. Usually we want someone to listen to us, but we need to make our own decisions. When a friend tells us what we should do, there's a subtle suggestion that they want to control our lives, and we subconsciously resent this. I have had to learn this in my relationship with my daughters. When they were little and would come home from school with a problem, I felt I had to solve it.

"Jimmy hit me in the back," my youngest said one day.

"Did you tell the teacher?" I asked.

"No . . ." she drawled, looking uncomfortable.

"Next time you tell the teacher, and don't play with him if he's going to hit. You tell him that you don't play with boys who hit . . ." and on and on. My daughter didn't want all this advice. All she wanted was her mom to listen and care. When we dump our advice on others, we're saying that we don't think they can handle the problem. This erodes their self-esteem and hurts relationships. So, remember, unless you are asked for advice, think very carefully before giving it.

Friendship, like all relationships, is built on trust. One of the most harmful things we can do to a friendship, McGinnis warns, is to tell someone else what our friend has told us in confidence. Remember when you were in the fifth or sixth grade and you told your best friend that you really liked a certain boy or girl? Some of us remember that friend telling someone else, who in turn told someone else, and soon it was all over the class. We were devastated, and our best friend lost our confidence.

McGinnis's fourth trait of a good listener is that he "completes the loop." A good listener will respond to the speaker. When we say something, we want our friend to give us some feedback, some acknowledgment, so that we know we've been heard. So, when listening to others, we must make an effort to really listen. It isn't easy because we are so readily distracted by things around us and by our own thoughts. It takes a conscious, concentrated effort to really listen to someone. To do this we must put our entire focus on the other person and forget ourselves for a time.

Lastly, McGinnis says to "show gratitude when someone confides." When someone confides in us it shows that they trust us. This is a great compliment, and we should let them know that we appreciate their trust. Our appreciation lets them feel secure and right about confiding in us, increasing trust and deepening our friendship even more.

DATING

Young people look forward to dating with excitement, expectation, and worry. Girls wonder if anyone will ask them out. Boys worry whether she will say yes. Girls become fixated on their appearance. Boys think and plan for that first car and a job, so they will have the money to show her a good time.

The easiest way to enter the dating scene is through group dates. By involving yourself in church groups or social groups of various kinds, you have the opportunity to meet friends of the opposite sex. Socializing in a group situation offers a more comfortable way of inter-acting than putting yourself in a one-to-one situation too quickly. It's like learning to swim. First you get used to the water. You stay in the shallow end of the pool with someone to support you. You learn to float, and then to breath properly, and finally to swim on your own. With a group you have friends of your own sex to support you. You gradually learn to carry on a conver-sation with someone of the opposite sex. As time passes, your experience socializing with others gives you confi-dence. You may meet someone special and want to go with them on a "real date." (Young people I've talked with don't view group dates as real dates. A real date is described as one boy, one girl, going out by themselves.)

There is no magic age at which everyone should start single-dating. Some ten-year-olds I know of are going to the movies together. Other young people I've known didn't start dating until after college. Only you know when the time is right for you. Many teens, however, let their friends push them into dating before they are ready. If all your friends are dating, you may feel pres-sured to find someone. You may need to prove that you are wanted by someone. You may need to show your friends that you, too, are desirable. It is uncomfortable to be different from your friends, so you may let your need to fit in push you into dating before you're really ready.

Laura, Cindy, and Barb were best friends. They did everything together. At a football game one night they met three boys who were also good friends. The boys invited them out for pizza after the game. Very quickly Laura and Cindy paired up with two of the boys. This left Barb with Derek, a boy she didn't feel comfortable with. Over the next few weeks Barb let her desire to be with her friends persuade her to go with the group to movies, on picnics, and to school games. At these outings she was always paired with Derek. After the first few dates she knew she didn't like Derek. He was egotistical and rude, and was always urging her to go all the way. She hated this, but she couldn't bring herself to break it off with him because she wanted to be part of the group. Finally, after Derek found he couldn't get what he wanted from Barb, he broke up with her. Barb felt terrible. Her friends were still dating, but she had no one. She tried not to let it bother her, but deep inside she felt completely rejected. To make matters worse, Laura and Cindy told her that Derek had been saying she was immature and frigid. Even though Barb knew why he was saying these things, they hurt her deeply. Every time she was with Laura and Cindy, they would talk about their boyfriends, share secrets, and giggle; they would run off and leave her whenever their boyfriends appeared. Barb began to think that maybe she should call Derek and try to get back together with him. Maybe she could learn to like him. Maybe if she gave him what he wanted things between them would improve.

Before Barb acted on her thoughts, an event occurred that saved her from making a terrible mistake. She was driving her friends to school one day when she was pulled over and ticketed for running a red light. It was her first ticket and she was shaken. She had to go to court for a hearing on her traffic violation, and she was scared.

"Will one of you go with me?" she asked.

"I can't," Laura said. "I have to study for an algebra test."

"Neither can I," Cindy added. "I'm babysitting."

A huge lump formed in Barb's throat that quickly heated into a ball of hot anger. This was the last straw. They had been treating her badly for weeks now. Excluding her, keeping secrets, and now this. This was the end. They could find their own rides to school from now on. It didn't matter that the girls had good excuses. It was rejection at a time when Barb couldn't handle it.

Barb ended their friendship at that moment, but it took her a long time to see that it wasn't because of her friends' refusal to go to court with her. She ended the friendship because of her feelings of rejection, hurt, and inadequacy.

Many young people find themselves in similar situations with friends when dating begins. Teens can avoid these kinds of problems by giving themselves value, worth, and love regardless of what others do or say. If another person doesn't recognize your value as a human being, it is their loss. Don't let their ignorance make a statement about you to you. You know yourself better than anyone else can. Valuing yourself will give you the strength to endure the hurts that people try to inflict on you. It doesn't mean you will never be hurt again. It means that you will be better able to deal with those hurts. One thing I have found that helps dispel hurt feelings may sound silly, but it works. When you are feeling especially vulnerable or unloved, sit down in front of a mirror. Stare into your eyes and project love from that deep part of you that is your higher self—the self that is a reflection of God. From that source you can renew yourself, strengthen yourself, and regain your confidence and well-being.

Teenagers date for all sorts of reasons, which may have nothing to do with liking the other person and wanting to be with him or her. Recognition is a big motivator, especially among young people who are just beginning to single-date. In American teen circles, status is given to those who begin dating first; therefore everyone is anxious for that first date. It doesn't matter at that point who you are dating. Just the news that you are going out with someone makes your friends notice you, and this makes you feel good.

Everyone loves a challenge, and we may go for the other person who seems unattainable. The thrill of the chase motivates some teens to do all sorts of silly or dumb things in order to capture the prize. For some, the fun ends when the prize is won. For others, the prize leads to a great awakening. They find that the person they so desperately wanted wasn't who they thought they were at all.

Most everyone who has done much dating has dated for the wrong reason. Terry breaks up with Brad, so Brad asks Terry's best friend out to get back at her. Joy accepts a date with Randy, to get close to Matt, his best friend. Amiee goes out with Greg because she wants to be seen in his new 240-sx Nissan. When we date someone for the wrong reason, we feel bad about it later. We know deeply that we have wronged them, and our self-esteem suffers.

When dating, many of us make one of two mistakes.

Either we hold back our feelings when we're with some-one we truly care for, or we smother the person with affection and become dependent and possessive. The best way is a middle ground between these two ap-proaches. If we have learned to love ourselves, we will be independent and confident. Then, when we're with someone we truly care for, we can let them know by being ourselves.

Everyone enjoys recognition and appreciates under-standing. We can let that special person know we care by giving him these things. We can let that person see that we accept him just as he is. We can be warm and affec-tionate without scaring him by declaring our undying love early in the relationship.

When we first start dating, we're not certain what is expected of us. We watch TV and movies and can some-times get distorted ideas of what we're supposed to do on dates. I remember the first boy I kissed introduced French kissing to me. I was naive and thought, "This must be how you're supposed to do it." I really didn't like it, but I didn't want anyone to think I didn't know how to kiss. So when the next boy I went out with started to kiss me, I responded the way I thought was the "right way." With a note of surprise in his voice, he said, "Oh . . . so you like to kiss like that!" I was devastated. It was clear that he hadn't expected French kissing.

I think the best guide to use when beginning to date is to date only those people you could have a great friendship with. Then treat each other as you would a good friend. Don't do anything that you think is "ex-pected," and take things slowly. If you don't feel right about something, pay attention to those feelings and discover what they are trying to tell you. If a dry period comes along when you don't have a date, accept it as being okay. Everyone doesn't have to have a date every weekend. Find and enjoy friends of the opposite sex whom you can have fun with, without getting serious. I think teenagers these days are much better at this than we were when I was their age. All of my daughters have had friendships with boys that were simply friendships and nothing more. They have also had friendships that developed into serious, loving relationships. My oldest daughter was good friends with her husband for three years before they started dating seriously. Then they dated for four years before getting married. They still consider themselves each other's best friend, although they maintain close ties with other friends of both sexes.

What if you go on a date that's a disaster? Should you avoid the other person for the rest of your life? If you can stand back and look at the evening objectively, you may be able to laugh. Don't take things too seriously when dating. Learn to laugh at yourself, and don't expect too much from the other person. Give them some slack and give yourself some, too. If you can lighten up, a disaster can turn into a fun evening even before it's over. If you can joke about it later, you might be able to go out again and have a great time. Much too often we take things too seriously when dating.

I thought I'd been stood up on the very first real date I had with the man I eventually married. He was working for the forest service and spent all week surveying in the Colorado mountains, returning to town around five o'clock on Fridays. Our date was for seven o'clock one Friday night. I was ready by 6:45 and was looking forward to the evening with excitement. I'd been wanting to date him for months, and this was to be the night.

Seven o'clock came and went, and he didn't show. The minutes ticked by, and I became more and more agitated. When he wasn't there by 7:30, I was angry. My niece was visiting us and wanted someone to take her home. I was so sure I'd been stood up that I was glad for an excuse to leave. Besides, it would serve him right if he came late to find me gone, so I left. Two minutes after I walked into my niece's house, my mother called to say he'd just phoned.

"What did he say?" I asked, kicking myself for leaving.

"Just that he'd call later," she reported.

I jumped in my car and drove home as fast as I could. I paced the floor waiting for his call. I worried that he'd been angry that I hadn't been there. Maybe he wouldn't call me back at all. Could I just stand there and hope and pray he'd call? Something told me I had to act. I picked up the phone and dialed his number. When he answered I said, "Well, where the heck are you, anyway?" He laughed and explained that the surveying crew had been recruited to help fight a forest fire and that they'd gotten back to town late. That was the beginning of a beautiful relationship that has lasted more than twenty-five years.

GOING STEADY

At some point after entering the dating scene, we may decide we'd like to go steady. Going steady takes the pressure off finding a date for Saturday night and gives young people a feeling of security. Going steady can be fun and relaxing, and a way of experiencing your first committed relationship. It also can lead to your first heartbreak if your steady doesn't feel the same commitment you do. It is good for a couple to get things straight with each other as to what going steady means to them. They should agree on the rules and the boundary lines when entering into this agreement. It is wise for them to agree to be honest with each other if they want the freedom to see someone else. It is far worse to find out that your steady is seeing someone else on the sly than to talk about it first and mutually agree to break up for a while.

What if your parents make a fuss about you going steady? Generally parents get worried when they see their teenager getting too serious too quickly. If their son or daughter begins spending all their time with their steady and stops seeing other friends, parents worry that the relationship is becoming too dependent, and that isn't healthy. A healthy, steady relationship does not exclude old friends or family. If you want to keep the excitement and fun in your relationship, don't spend every possible moment together. When you're together too much you begin to take each other for granted and conflict is more likely to occur. Parents will generally not object to your going steady as long as you have established trust with them and don't become obsessive about your relationship.

Whether you are just dating or going steady, expect to be treated by your partner with consideration and respect. Know that you deserve good treatment and don't accept anything less. If you find yourself with someone with a bad attitude, someone who drives too fast, uses drugs or alcohol, or doesn't control his temper, get away from him. These kinds of people will bring problems on themselves, and you don't want to be with them when they do. You may believe you can help them, but chances are these are problems they will need to resolve on their own. It's better to sit home alone on Saturday night than go out with someone like this.

LOVING

You're in love. It's exciting and fun and, when your loved one returns your love, you feel aglow, happy. The feeling of being in love is special. It can also be fleeting.

Falling in love is a phrase that is used very lightly during the teenage years. Usually what we are really feeling is attraction for another person. Since this feeling involves many different emotions, we tend to think we are in love. The problem is that our love is conditional and therefore very unreliable. We love this person until he does something we don't like. We have difficulty separating ourselves from our loved one, and we want him to do what we'd like him to do. This is called controlling. No one likes to be controlled. If you want to end a relationship quickly, try controlling the other person.

If we really love another person we will encourage their independence. No one can be happy if they are dependent on someone else. Dependency kills self-esteem. If we truly love another we will give him some space in the relationship. Real love not only appreciates the other person's individuality and independence but encourages it. If we create some space and allow the one we care for to be his own person, he will love us for it.

A genuinely loving relationship cannot endure without commitment. Commitment is like a promise or a pledge that two people make to each other. We can promise each other to be open and honest, to be understanding and reliable. If we are engaged, we should commit to being faithful to each other and trusting each other. Commitment is the glue that holds a relationship together when problems arise or misunderstandings occur.

Many times when we "fall in love" we let our own needs suffer while trying to fulfill all the needs and wants of our loved one. We must remember to always see ourselves as individuals and not just as part of a couple. We must recognize our own feelings and not suppress them in order to make our loved one happy. If we will respect ourselves and love ourselves first, we will then be better able to love another.

WHAT LOVING ANOTHER IS NOT

Being in love or going steady does not mean that we own the other person or that she owns us. If we can't let the one we love have interests outside our relationship, if we can't give her the freedom she needs to discover herself, if we can't allow her other friendships, then we don't really love her. Instead of loving her, we are dependent on her, and we are so afraid of losing her that we hold on with a deathlike grip.

Being in love doesn't mean that you have to agree on everything. It's okay to disagree—to have different opinions about things. The important thing is to respect each other's opinions. We can be different and that's okay. We don't have to make our loved one conform to our own image. If we truly love her we will allow her to have her own ideas, beliefs, and ambitions, and we can expect her to allow us ours.

Being in love doesn't mean that we've found someone

to fulfill our every need. No one else can fulfill our needs. Only we can do that. If we are looking for our sweetheart to fill our needs, we will be very disappointed. Love means that we help the other fulfill his or her own needs by providing support, freedom, and encouragement.

If we look at the person we've fallen in love with as a very special friend, the same suggestions apply to love as to friendship. We all have the same needs. We all need to be wanted, appreciated, and accepted just as we are. We need discipline in our lives and a sense of achievement. We need reality born of honesty with ourselves and our friends. And we need understanding, cooperation, and support from those we care about. Surprisingly enough, whether it's in friendship or in love, when we focus on giving in a relationship rather than receiving, we will find our needs fulfilled and the love we want flowing effortlessly into our lives.

CHAPTER III

Self-Discipline

From the time we are small children, life seems to be shoving, pushing, and prodding us toward self-discipline. When we can't find our shoes amidst piles of clothes, books, and toys, we know it's because we haven't cleaned our room. When we go to the dentist and discover that we have a cavity, we know it's because we didn't take proper care of our teeth. When we get a bad grade on our report card, we know that we should have done the homework or studied more.

Why do we fight doing what we know we should do when the penalties can be so severe? When we become teenagers, self-discipline becomes more important than ever, but it seems that the fight becomes even fiercer. Bedrooms that were fairly well kept when we were younger now resemble scenes from a war movie. Musical instruments that we practiced conscientiously a few years ago are neglected or ignored entirely.

Maybe we need to understand that self-discipline is simply controlling oneself and thereby bringing order to one's life. As long as we refuse to control our behavior, we cause ourselves great problems. Parents would much rather have their teenagers discipline themselves, but when teens don't get out of bed in time for school, don't get their homework done, don't care for their clothes and other things that belong to them, parents are likely to respond by taking control away from their children. Grounding and restrictions are generally the first ways parents deal with problems. Teenagers hate this, but in reality by not accepting self-discipline they are giving personal control of their lives away.

Self-discipline is taking responsibility for ourselves— for our behavior, our feelings, and our attitudes. It's planning ahead, scheduling our priorities, not according to what we want to do but according to what needs to be done to bring order, harmony, success, and fulfillment to our lives. A counselor at San Diego State University told me that the major problem of incoming freshmen is time management. She said if, in his first semester at the university, a student doesn't learn how to prioritize—that is, how to schedule his activities according to their importance toward his education—he will not remain in college very long.

A self-disciplined individual takes full responsibility for achieving success. He also recognizes the part he has played in his own failures. He doesn't look for someone else to blame. He looks at his failures as learning experiences and accepts accountability for them. In this way he ensures himself personal growth from the lesson he has learned. When we accept that we are responsible for the quality of our lives, we will achieve self-discipline.

Self-discipline is essential for solving life's problems. We cannot solve anything until we are willing to recognize the problem as belonging to us and to accept responsibility for solving it ourselves. Without self-discipline there can be no success and no fulfillment in life.

Total self-discipline is a lifelong struggle. We start with little things like keeping our rooms clean and getting our homework done. As we become more self-disciplined, we are able to accept more responsibilities—a job, perhaps, or driving a car. With each step we take, another arises to be mastered. We learn to tell ourselves no. *No, you can't have that second piece of cake. No, you can't afford the suit and a new pair of shoes, too.* We learn to manage our time and direct our activities. Young people find that being an adult demands wise choices and that these choices always require self-discipline.

By being self-disciplined, that is, doing the things that we are responsible for, we simplify our lives, create peace and well-being around us, and make possible options and opportunities that would otherwise not occur. Let's say Erin makes a decision to start keeping her bedroom clean, and to make sure that her clothes, shoes, school things, and fun things are organized and cared for. Her life becomes simpler because she always knows where things are. She's created a peaceful atmosphere around her because no one is yelling at her to do these things. She has a sense of well-being because she is in control of her surroundings and her behavior. Also her mom is more likely to let her have people over to spend the night or to let her go somewhere. The self-discipline that she practices in regard to her room and possessions will transfer to other areas of her life. Soon she finds that the same benefits are lifting these areas to greater satisfaction. Opportunities for trips, scholarships, or other good things begin to come her way.

LEARNING SELF-DISCIPLINE

Learning self-discipline starts with getting good, consistent, fair discipline from our parents. At a very young age we find that we can't have everything we want. At first we resist being told no. Around the age of two we begin to struggle with our parents as we first experience discipline. This period has been described as the terrible twos. Some children resist more than others, but eventually persistent, loving parents will train their children to accept that the universe does not revolve around them and their desires. Quickly following this stage parents begin to ask their child to discipline himself. This usually first occurs when the child begins toilet training. The parents are now asking their child to be responsible for one of his own natural bodily needs. As the years pass, good parents will help the child to accept responsibility for more and more of his own life.

Parents can do only so much, however. Ultimately, the decision to become self-disciplined has to be made by the individual. Even when we recognize that self-discipline will make our lives more fulfilling, we fight it. Why is this so? I think it's a matter of experiencing the need for it, recognizing the benefits, and then making a conscious choice.

My second daughter was seventeen and had owned her car only a few months when it broke down thirty miles from home at one o'clock in the morning. Her father dragged himself out of bed, got dressed, and went to her rescue. When he couldn't locate the problem or start her car, he arranged to have it towed. The next morning they found out that her engine had burned up from a lack of oil.

"Didn't I show you how to check your oil when you first got the car?" her dad asked.

"I guess so . . ." she drawled, looking as though she wanted to hide under the kitchen table.

"You guess so! You know good and well I explained

how to check the oil, the water, and the belts and hoses," he sputtered, trying to control his temper.

"I know, but I forgot." Her voice was beginning to quiver.

"That's no excuse," he barked. "You were responsible for maintaining your car and now *you* are responsible for having it repaired."

She had been working at Mrs. Fields Cookies since she'd turned sixteen and had saved slightly more than the $1,500 that it cost to have the car repaired. Withdrawing her hard-earned money and giving it to the mechanic was a difficult but valuable lesson in responsibility and self-discipline. That experience made her see, for the first time, the severe consequences we must pay when we ignore our responsibilities. Once we understand this, we can start becoming masters of ourselves. By overcoming the human tendency toward seeking the easy way, we will transcend our lower nature and begin to grow spiritually.

OVERCOMING BLOCKS TO SELF-DISCIPLINE

One way young people can learn self-discipline is from observing their own parents. Loving parents who demonstrate on a daily basis their own self-discipline provide good role models. However, not everyone has loving, nurturing, self-disciplined parents, and so for some, the opportunity for learning self-discipline is much more limited.

For an intelligent, thinking young person the negative role model provided by some parents can be a powerful motivator for self-discipline. Homes with undisciplined parents are characterized by problems. There

may be problems with alcohol or with money. The father may not be able to keep a job; the mother may
forget to pay bills or keep appointments. Whatever di-
rection the problems take, they result in a family unit
that doesn't function well. If a teen can recognize that
not all parents are like his, and that order and harmony
are the norm in some other homes, he may be able to
deduce that his parents' lack of self-discipline may be
the cause of their problems. If the teenager can make
this connection, it will be possible for him to take control
of his own life and live it differently than his parents
have lived theirs. It isn't easy to overcome the habits
we've adopted from our parents, but, with work, it is
possible.

Many times we lack confidence in our ability to complete a homework project or some other task, so we
procrastinate—we put off starting until the last possible
moment. What we don't understand is that it takes getting into the project to give us the confidence to know
we can handle it. Have you ever heard the saying, "Once
begun, half done"? It's strange, but the hardest part of
any job is getting started.

LOOKING AT WORK DIFFERENTLY

Children are wonderfully spontaneous, fun-loving, en-
thusiastic individuals with a great gusto for life. With all
the fun, exciting things there are to do, it's not surprising that they aren't eager to stop and clean their rooms,
do their chores, or practice their musical instruments.
Before the teenage years even begin, we start to struggle
with our parents about these things. But how long we
struggle is up to us. As we grow and mature, we learn to

see beyond the present moment. We begin to see that there is more to life than just having fun or being entertained. The first time we experience the satisfaction that comes from a job well done, we realize that work can bring a kind of fulfillment that just having fun can never give us. Once we experience this fulfillment and understand that it comes directly from our willingness to delay our fun, and choose to work instead, we have made a giant step forward in self-discipline. The willingness to set aside what we want to do, in order to accomplish what we need to do, is a sign of maturity.

Many things—in fact, most things of lasting worth—do not come easily. Effort is required, but sometimes we don't have enough love for ourselves to exert this effort. Remember our definition of love—to help oneself or another grow spiritually. To do this means we will have to exert effort. In other words, real love takes work. The opposite of work is laziness. Therefore, it's our laziness that causes our lack of self-discipline and this lack holds us back spiritually.

No one would disagree that watching television is easier than cleaning your room, learning to play the piano, teaching yourself to type, or any other activity that takes work, perseverance, and commitment. However, when we've finished watching the program, the good feeling—the feeling of pleasure—diminishes very quickly. When we spend time working on a project or improving our skills and talents, there will be a feeling of satisfaction that will stay with us much longer. We will be filling our need for accomplishment, which will increase our self-esteem. When we live our lives only for pleasure, we find that pleasure alone soon leads to boredom. Then we start trying to find other things that will bring us the pleasure we want. A teenager who is into pleasure gratification may sink into exciting (but dangerous) behavior. He may get into drugs, alcohol, sexual experimentation, even stealing or setting fires. Pleasure is an elusive thing. The more we go after it, the more energy and ingenuity it takes to find it. Of course, there must be times when we relax, have fun, and play, too. But play must be controlled, by us, for our own well-being. Too much work may make Brad a dull boy, but too much play makes him dangerous.

We need to look at work differently—as a privilege, an opportunity, an expression of our individuality and free will. When we begin to look at work in this way, we will find a kind of fulfillment and satisfaction that nothing else in life can bring. We will experience life that is full, rich, and overflowing with possibilities. When we let go of our desire for pleasure, stop seeking the easy way, and choose instead those things that lead to fulfillment, a strange thing occurs. We begin to find pleasure in the work we are doing. The satisfaction and sense of accomplishment make us feel happy, involved in life, and fulfilled. When we feel this way, we are healthy, both physically and spiritually.

Choosing Responsibility

Have you ever noticed the different feeling you get when the job you've completed was one of your own choosing rather than one that your parents made you do? When you see something that needs to be done and choose to do it without being told, you get more satisfaction afterward. This is because you are controlling your own behavior rather than submitting to someone else's control. In other words, you are taking the responsibility yourself for getting the job done. Not only do you feel better about the work you've accomplished, but your parents are much more appreciative than if they've had to yell at you for a week to get it done. By accepting responsibility for your own "things," you are claiming your own freedom. You are becoming an independent, free being with mature attitudes and behaviors.

Choosing responsibility for our life involves accepting responsibility for our problems. This does not come naturally. It's easier to blame someone else, or try to hide from our problems, or ignore them and hope they will go away by themselves.

Josh and Larry were having a tough time in chemistry. They had both gotten D's on the first test and felt completely lost. Their teacher zipped through his lectures and never allowed enough time for questions. He would give them their assignment in the lab, then go into his office, leaving them alone for an hour to work on their own. Both boys had the same problem but chose to react to it differently. Larry complained a lot. He blamed the teacher for not teaching the subject well. He excused himself from finishing some of the labs because the teacher wasn't there to help him. After failing the second test, Larry dropped the class and angrily blamed the teacher. Josh, on the other hand, began looking for other solutions to his problem. He knew that if he dropped the class it would put him behind. He needed the class, and he didn't want to create more problems for himself later. He didn't like the teacher any better than Larry did, but he was determined not to let one teacher sway him from his goal. Josh went to the tutoring center at school and arranged for a tutor to help him three hours every week. He also enlisted his dad's help in the evenings when he was working on the problems. During the labs, when he had a question he would go into the teacher's office and ask for help. Whatever it took, Josh was determined to pass the class. His perseverance and determination got him a B out of the class, and he continued on through school with his plans undisturbed. There may be times when dropping a class is the best solution to a problem, but make sure it's the best solution, not just the easiest.

Keeping Discipline Flexible

Once in a while a person will come along who takes to self-discipline zealously. While self-discipline is needed, we don't want to become so self-disciplined that we become rigid. David was the eldest of four children. He had always been given much responsibility and had a good sense of self-worth. His parents trusted him and he matured early. Along with his maturity, he became acutely self-disciplined. His friends would come by and want him to go to the beach, but he would turn them down because he had planned to wash his car that afternoon. If someone was using the computer at the moment he had planned to write his report, he would be furious. His girlfriend broke a date with him because her uncle had arrived unexpectedly after returning from China, and David couldn't handle the change in plans. "You can go back to China with your uncle for all I care," he yelled, slamming the phone down.

If a person becomes self-disciplined to an extreme, they may become rigid and inflexible. Individuals must remember to use good judgment and look at each situation as unique. Developing the ability to be flexible while maintaining our self-discipline is very important. We must balance our daily plans, as well as our purpose and aims for the future, with being able to enjoy the present and act spontaneously.

Discipline provides us with attitudes we need to solve the problems that occur in our life. Discipline doesn't come naturally to us. None of us are born as self-disciplined individuals. Just as we must learn to discipline our natural bodily functions (by learning to use the toilet), we must learn to discipline our behavior. We must do what we know needs to be done before doing what we want to do. It all boils down to making a conscious choice—choosing not necessarily what comes naturally, but choosing to do the things that will bring us fulfillment, peace, and spiritual growth.

CHAPTER IV

Pitfalls and Mistakes

The greatest assurance of a successful journey through life is a clear vision of our destination—where we want to go and what we hope to accomplish. If that sounds like a cliché, it is nevertheless one of life's great truths. Equally true is that many, if not most, of the obstacles that lie in our way are of our own making—those self-defeating habits and preconceived notions that lead us into serious pitfalls and mistakes. With vision and understanding we can learn to steer clear of these hazards when we encounter them in our lives.

EXPECTING PERFECTION

One mistake many of us make is expecting ourselves to be perfect. Actually this attitude is very egotistical. We must allow ourselves to make mistakes because they are valuable for our spiritual growth. This doesn't mean that we shouldn't strive to put forth our best effort, but if we know that we've done that, then we must accept what comes. We must love ourselves regardless of the outcome.

Why are we so hard on ourselves when we fail? Why are some of us incapable of accepting defeat in anything? Winning is so important to us. Losing is abominable. Needing to win is directly related to how we feel about ourselves in the deep recesses of our being.

When I was little, some of my first memories were of my older sister, who was a teenager. She seemed so glamorous when she'd get dressed up, with her long, blond hair styled just so. She always had lots of dates, and I would watch as she'd sweep out of the house on the arm of her beau. When I became a teenager, I felt I never quite measured up to the way she had been. I never appreciated my own uniqueness and felt instead that I had to prove something to be worthy. I can remember wanting something badly, praying for it, and ending the prayer with "not for self-glory but for self-worth." What I didn't understand was that I was already worthy. We don't have to earn our worth. It is a gift from God, but until we recognize it and allow ourselves to receive it, we will never have it. Thinking that we have to do something to gain worthiness is a fallacy. When we understand that self-worth is simply recognizing the worth or value that we already have, we will be paving the way for our success.

For many years, the only time I would feel good about myself was when I'd win at something. Whether it was getting A's on my report card, winning games, or attracting a new boyfriend, feeling good about me became entirely dependent on my successes. When I'd win, I figured I must be okay, after all. But when I'd lose, I'd get depressed and feel terrible about myself.

If how we feel about ourselves is dependent on being perfect, always winning, or never making mistakes, we will never be happy. No one wins all the time. No one is perfect. We must learn to accept our mistakes as a natural part of living. We must look at mistakes as lessons that we need to learn in order to grow spiritually. Losing is just as important as winning. If we never lost, think what egotists we'd be. No one could stand to be around us. The important lesson of humility could never be learned if we always won. We really should be thankful when we lose for the insight that it gives us about our own nature. The insight can come, however, only when we recognize that our anger, frustration, and hurt are outward signs of a deeper unacceptance of ourselves as we are. Seeing this, we can then make a conscious choice to accept our losses, our imperfections, and our mistakes as part of the valuable experiences that make up our life.

PRECONCEIVED IDEAS

If we reflect upon our childhood judiciously, we will discover opinions and ideas that we have formed about life as a direct result of things that have happened to us. These ideas have become our preconceived notions about life, and they don't necessarily reflect the truth.

When Cindy was in the first grade, she had a teacher who was overweight to the point of being obese. Mrs. Smith was also authoritarian, overly strict, and humorless. Cindy shook every time the large woman got angry and raised her voice. Each morning Cindy would quietly slip into her desk, trying her best to not be noticed by her teacher. For an entire year Cindy felt dominated and intimidated by Mrs. Smith. She felt oppressed by her temper, by her loud voice, and especially by her size. Somewhere in that uncomfortable year Cindy decided that fat people were unkind and were to be avoided.

The August before eighth grade Cindy moved with her family to another state. Next door to Cindy's new home lived a girl the same age as Cindy. Jenna had a pretty face, long brown hair, and a weight problem. She wasn't fat exactly, but she was overweight for her height. During the few weeks before school started, Jenna tried to make friends with Cindy. She asked her to go shopping, to go bike riding, and to attend her church youth group. Cindy turned her down each time. She took an instant dislike to Jenna and was sure they could never be friends. When school started, Cindy was shocked to learn that Jenna was a cheerleader and one of the most popular girls at school. Cindy told herself she didn't care and began looking for other friends.

When Cindy turned sixteen she began looking for a job. Not many of the stores were hiring, and each application she filled out was met with the same "We're not hiring right now but we'll keep your application on file." One day Cindy heard of a new record shop opening in the area. She'd always dreamed of working in a record shop, so she hurried down to put in her application. She was told that they were looking for people and that if she'd come back the next day the manager would be there. Cindy could hardly wait for her interview and was excited when she returned the following day. She entered the store and asked for the manager. Soon a very large, overweight woman came out from the back and asked Cindy to have a seat in her small office. A sudden feeling of terror slithered up Cindy's spine as the woman began asking her questions. Her hands began to shake, and she avoided the woman's gaze. She felt herself stiffly answering the woman's questions. After fifteen minutes the woman said she'd let Cindy know and walked her to the door.

The next day the manager of the record store called and left a message that the position had been filled with another applicant. Cindy was hurt and angry, and her first impulse was to blame the heavyset woman. That night after she'd had time to cool off, she lay in bed replaying in her mind the details of her interview. She had known all along that it hadn't gone well. She remembered her nervousness and the way she'd answered the woman's questions. She felt horrible about losing the opportunity she'd been so excited about. As she made a thorough assessment of her conduct during the interview, she thought back to other times she had reacted with hostility toward heavy people. She thought of Jenna, who had tried to be her friend and whom she'd treated so badly. Cindy gradually began to realize that her ideas about heavy people had caused her to react the way she had—ideas that had begun in the first grade when Mrs. Smith had terrified her.

Cindy had let her preconceived ideas distort her reality. She had thought her perceptions were real, but they were warped by a belief formed long ago. She was limiting herself and her own opportunities by letting that belief direct her actions. When we let our preconceived ideas direct our actions, we cause ourselves problems.

When problems arise in our lives we would be wise to ask ourselves if preconceived ideas have played a part in creating the problem. With truthful self-examination we may discover that the difficulty isn't just happening to us, but that we have actually played a part in creating it. It isn't easy to examine our motivations and to look at our problems objectively. Finding the truth demands that we put aside our preconceived notions and view our problem with honesty. We must be willing to let go of our need to defend ourselves and be able to look at

our problem with some detachment, like a scientist examining slides under a microscope.

Cindy's beliefs caused her to expect heavy people to
be unkind. This caused her to interpret what they said
and how they behaved wrongly. If we can drop our past
experiences and look at each event with the openness of
a young child, viewing it as part of the moment we are
in and not as part of any previous experience, then we
will be able to see things as they are. In other words, we
will see reality.

DISHONESTY

Among the things that are hurtful to our spirit is dishonesty in any and all of its forms. Lying and cheating
generally begin in childhood. They are motivated by
fear—fear of disapproval or fear of punishment. Billy
breaks his mom's candy dish and hides it behind the
couch. Then he denies it when she questions him. Milly
writes her spelling words on her arm because she needs
the grade to get her parents' approval.

Usually children get caught when they lie or cheat,
and they find the consequence to be even more severe
than the thing they had originally feared. This, along
with the family values instilled in the child, will cause
him to refrain from his dishonest behavior. Sometimes,
however, a child will get away with lying or cheating,
and the behavior will persist. Relief at not getting caught
is followed by either guilt or a sort of high caused by the
absence of respect for the person lied to or cheated.
This may be true if the child has not bonded with his
parents or if family values do not include honesty. On
the other hand, if the family unit is controlled by an

authoritarian figure who demands honesty, the child can get a euphoric feeling from getting away with it. His lying or cheating can become a habit, even an addiction.

The child, as he grows into adolescence, is encouraged toward even more dishonesty by feelings of rebellion and the pleasure he gets each time he deceives someone. He may begin to lie about things that don't matter, steal things he doesn't want, just for the kick he gets out of it. His behavior may become habitual and begin to control him more than he controls his behavior.

Steven was such a boy. When Steven was a child his father was a harsh disciplinarian. If Steven didn't do everything his father told him to, he was in for a severe lashing. Steven began to find ways of deceiving his father. His mother, who was abused by Steven's father as well, became his accomplice in these deceptions, and they would laugh behind his father's back at how they had fooled him. Lying soon became a habit with Steven. When he started high school, he found that lying and cheating would get him the grades, the girls, and the attention he enjoyed so much. Steven always had at least two girls thinking they were his steady at one time. He made up stories about a rich grandfather who had left him beach property and a huge trust fund. He became a master manipulator with his stories and fantasies. During his senior year his lies began caving in on each other. Some of his old girlfriends got to talking and found out that he'd been seeing them all at the same time. Word began to spread about his character. One teacher caught him cheating and warned other teachers to watch him. One after another his dishonest activities were discovered. Finally, he was suspended from school and abandoned by his friends.

Steven knew he had a problem, but he wasn't willing to do anything about it. He ended up joining the Navy and leaving town, which was his way of running away from his problem. However, since the problem was within him, he took it along, and it continued to create more and more difficulties in his life. He lived in a world of illusion, created by his unwillingness to break habits he had formed as a child.

Steven's dishonesty has hurt him spiritually. Hurting ourselves spiritually is the most serious kind of hurt that we can inflict upon ourselves. Lying, cheating, and other forms of dishonesty create consequences that must be dealt with. They follow the law of cause and effect. God doesn't punish us for our sins. The consequences of our sin is our punishment. If we cannot find the courage to confront our shortcomings and mistakes, and understand where they came from, we will never discover who we are. The wounds we've inflicted on our spirit must be dealt with in order for us to progress spiritually.

Fun or Folly

The party was just getting started. Jake's parents were away for the weekend, and he'd passed the word at school that day: "Party—my house—8:00 sharp." At first everything went great. Music blasted from the tape deck in the family room, pizza and soft drinks covered the bar leading to the kitchen, and carefree teens congregated about the room. As the minutes ticked by a few more kids dropped in; some of them Jake barely knew. After a while some of the kids began to feel bored. "What this party needs is some beer," one boy shouted. "Beer—beer—beer," several others began to chant. Jake wanted everyone to have a good time, he wanted to be liked and accepted by all the kids, so he dashed out to the big, old refrigerator in the garage and dragged out four six-packs his dad had stored there. After all the beer was gone, one of the boys spotted some hard liquor in the bar. Jake knew he'd be in big trouble when his dad found out about the beer, and he didn't want to let his friends have the liquor. But how could he tell them no. They'd think he was a wimp. Everyone was having a good time, and one bottle couldn't hurt. One bottle led to two, two became three. As the evening wore on, things got completely out of hand. Jake's house was completely trashed, holes were burned in the sofa, drinks were spilled on the carpet and the furniture. Two end tables were broken, and the sliding glass door was cracked. None of this, however, even compared to the tragedy that followed later that night. One of Jake's best friends ended up in intensive care with severe head injuries after crashing his new, red Firebird into a parked car.

When we let being part of the group overshadow what we know is right, when we let ourselves be carried away with the fun of the moment with no thought about the possible consequences, we are not acting responsibly. When our irresponsibility causes pain and suffering for others, we are hurting ourselves spiritually. We can never run away from spiritual wounds. We can't hide from them. We can't ignore them. One way we can heal a spiritual wound is by making amends. This is why we often see people who were drug addicts working in anti-drug efforts. People who were thieves may end up helping to teach communities how to protect themselves from break-ins. These people know in their hearts that healing takes place through rectification—setting things right.

Though it isn't strictly confined to adolescence, teens seem to be more vulnerable to stepping over the line between fun and folly. Our very nature when we are teenagers makes us susceptible. Through awareness, however, and an effort to transcend our adolescent nature we can protect ourselves from spiritual injury and trauma.

ADOPTING AN IMAGE THAT IS NOT YOU

When Tina's parents decided to move the family from the East Coast to the West Coast, Tina was angry. She loved her school, her friends, her neighborhood, and her life, and she didn't want to move. When Tina entered her new school in California, she was still angry. She could think of nothing but moving back to New York. When the kids tried to get acquainted with her, Tina rebuffed them. She had no interest in making new friends. She thought constantly of her old friends in New York. She wrote letters to them every day. She dreamed of going back to her old home, her old neighborhood. She rejected all attempts by her parents, her teachers, and the new kids to help her adjust to her new situation.

After six months passed, Tina finally saw that wishing she could return to New York was futile. Her family was living in California now, and there was nothing that was going to change that. She finally decided that she wanted to make some new friends. Now, however, the other kids were not receptive to her overtures of friendship. They had made up their minds that Tina was unfriendly, distant, and a snob. They wanted nothing to do with her. Tina had a problem, and she didn't know what to do about it. What would you do if you were Tina?

Rather than confront the problem head-on, and meet their rejection with understanding, rather than persisting in her effort to change their minds about her by being friendly, warm, and generous in spirit, Tina let herself be hurt more by their rejection. Finally one day she saw some girls at the mall dressed all in black. They had strange hairdos, dyed weird colors. These girls captured her attention, and she was fascinated by their camaraderie, the closeness they seemed to share as a group. Impulsively she turned into a shop and bought an entire black outfit. When she showed up at school Monday with her new clothes, her dyed hair, and her hopeful expectations, she got a lot of recognition. She still wasn't accepted in the way she wanted to be, but the recognition was certainly a lot better than being ignored.

Tina continued to wear the dark clothes when she started high school the next year. She found a few other kids wearing black and became friends with them. Now she belonged to a group, and she felt good about herself at last. As her high school years passed, many of the kids she'd hung out with as a freshman dropped out of school, some transferred to other schools, and some just quit wearing black. Tina, however, couldn't seem to give up the black clothes because now they had become part of her image. She could only see herself in black. If her mom made her put on a pink dress, she felt extremely uncomfortable. The pink dress wasn't just a pink dress, it was a threat to her ego. Wearing it threatened to destroy the image that she had created of herself, and since she could only see herself one way, anything else was like death.

Sometimes we hang on to an image that we've impulsively created of ourselves for years and years. Learning that the image is not us, the body we inhabit is not us, and the mind we use to get ourselves so screwed up is not us takes many of us a lifetime, maybe many lifetimes. The part of us that is eternal has no image. The part of us that lasts is pure spirit. The things in our heart, not the clothes on our body, are the real us.

DRUGS AND ALCOHOL

There are really only two reasons why teenagers get involved in taking drugs, drinking alcohol, or other destructive behavior. One is the fear of rejection, and the other is the need to escape emotional pain. When we haven't fully accepted ourselves, our need for acceptance can block our will to act responsibly and say no. When we're not sure yet who we are, our search for identity can lead us to self-destruct before we've had a chance to find out. Our desire to fit in, to be part of the group—as in the case of Jake and his ill-fated party—can make us go along when we know deeply we should not.

Some young people have great problems in their lives—abusive parents, divorced parents, and dysfunctional families, to name a few. These teens may find that drugs or alcohol offer temporary relief from these problems. When we are suffering pain, whether physical or emotional, it is natural for us to seek a way out, and we can easily be fooled into believing we've found the solution. Drugs and alcohol, however, are not the answer.

They only serve to block the teenager's progress to the inevitable confrontation that he must undertake toward his problems. It's much easier to avoid problems, however, than to confront them. This is why many of us will spend years ignoring problems before we finally realize that we will not be happy until we confront and resolve them.

The teen who has never learned to value himself, who looks to others for his sense of self-worth, may be susceptible to the urgings of his peers to join in their drinking. Many young people have the idea that alcohol is harmless and will help them to relax and have fun. Maybe they have seen their parents drink. They've watched beer ads on television that make it seem that drinking is the way to have fun. Our society has condoned alcohol as socially acceptable, while at the same time telling teenagers they can't drink until they're twenty-one. This makes alcohol even more attractive as it becomes the grown-up thing to do.

The fact is that alcohol is a drug. It alters our thinking process and loosens our inhibitions. It blocks our ability to think rationally and distinguish fun from folly. Studies have shown that teens who drink alcohol are more likely to take other drugs while under the influence of alcohol. Teens who drink are less able to control their sexual or aggressive feelings. Automobile accidents in which the driver has been drinking alcohol are the leading cause of death among fifteen- to twenty-four-year-olds in America.

In a study done at the University of Missouri, it was found that four-fifths of adult alcoholics began drinking before the age of eighteen. The average age these users began drinking was thirteen. Our habits become our lives, and if we get into the habit of drinking regularly as teenagers, we are likely to become addicted at some point. High school students who begin drinking on a daily basis begin missing school and have a high probability of dropping out. This leads to an array of problems that eats away at self-esteem, and the teen may even be driven to try suicide.

Many teens have had the heartbreaking experience of watching a friend destroy himself through the use of illegal drugs. Usually the young person who starts smoking pot will soon be trying other drugs. It is not unusual to see a teenager on a TV talk show listing five, six, or seven drugs he has used in his short life. When young people get into heavy drug use, everything else goes out the window. Social development stops, mental and spiritual evolution cease, and growth toward adulthood comes to an abrupt halt. Until the teen is ready to face his problem with honesty and take responsibility for his own health, he will not be able to continue on his life's path.

Illegal drugs account for millions of ruined lives every year. Those young people who use alcohol or drugs are responsible for the tragedies they cause in their own lives as well as the tragedies they cause in the lives of others. Shooting victims, auto accident victims, and their families cry for an end to the destructive use of alcohol and drugs. But for many teens the need to be popular forces them to ignore the message. The impression they make on others becomes their only concern. They let their vision narrow to include only those things that will help them fit in.

There are other young people today, however, who are more in tune with the whole picture. They have heard the message and have chosen to resist when others urge them to join the crowd. These are kids who have learned to think for themselves and be themselves no matter what others may say.

Groups of teens are forming to fight drug and alcohol abuse in their own way. Just as young people have gotten the message about the destructive effects of smoking, they are increasing their awareness of the tragedy and devastation caused by alcohol and drug use. An organization called Pride is one nationwide group of teenagers helping teenagers fight drug abuse. By teaching young people to feel good about themselves and to develop a sense of self-worth, Pride empowers troubled teens to stand up to the pressure from others to use drugs. Just Say No, Youth to Youth, and Students Against Drunk Driving (SADD) are other nationwide teen groups that are having a positive effect on the fight against teenage drug use in this country. Though the problem is far from over, teenagers in every part of the nation are seeing that they have power over their own lives, that they can choose to exercise that power and create a happy life for themselves and their friends.

SEX

Teenagers today have more pressure on them to have sex and to avoid having sex than at any other time in history. It is very confusing. Sex can be the most deeply fulfilling of experiences or it can be the most terrible of experiences. So how can teenagers sort it all out and decide what is best for them?

No one can tell another person when it is right for him to become sexually active. A teenager has to be able to liberate himself from all the pressures and decide what is right for him. The important thing to remember is to use wisdom, love (not emotional love but real love), and intelligent judgment when making that choice. Your decision should be preceded by a great deal of thought and self-examination. You must be able to understand your motives for wanting to be intimate with that other person. Your motives must be so crystal clear in your mind that you have no hesitation or question about taking this big step.

How do you know when a certain person is the "right" one for you? There is no way of knowing without first experiencing the friendship of many young people of the opposite sex. Find out what different guys and girls are like and how they feel about things. See what makes them tick. It takes experience, along with your natural growth and maturity, for you to know what you want in a partner. Finding that special person can't be rushed. Hoping and wishing for that special person to come into your life doesn't work either. What works is being the kind of person you are looking for. In this way you will attract the same kind of person. Be receptive to new friendships, and take your time in establishing relationships. Recognizing that special person takes getting to know them beyond their projected image and seeing what motivates them.

If, after a great deal of self-examination, you find that your motive for entering into an intimate relationship is to get something for yourself or to gain in any way, you are not being motivated by love. If you want to do it to live up to the expectations of your friends or to feel more grown-up, your motivation is wrong. Wanting to be intimate has everything to do with giving of yourself and nothing to do with gaining. You must be as concerned with what is good for the other person as with what is good for you.

"Ben's been pressuring me to sleep with him," Kerri told her older sister after a particularly bad fight with their mother. "And I think I'm going to."

"Don't be stupid," her sister warned. "You sleep with him and you'll end up getting pregnant, like I did."

"He makes me feel special though. Like I'm somebody."

Kerri was one of five children still living at home with their mother, who was on welfare. She shared a bedroom with her older sister, Amanda, and Amanda's six-year-old son, as well as a younger sister.

"He'll make you feel special until he gets what he wants," Amanda said bitterly. "Then he'll take off and leave you with a child to raise."

"Ben wouldn't do that."

"I didn't think James would leave me either. Get smart, Kerri! Don't make the same mistake I did."

"I don't know. If I don't give in, I'm afraid he'll find someone else. I need him, Mandy."

"If he really loves you, Kerri, he'll wait. Don't let yourself get seduced by promises of love. Do you want to still be living with Mama when you're twenty-four, depending on her to care for your child so you can work at a minimum-wage, get-nowhere job?"

No, that wasn't what Kerri wanted. She had dreamed of going to college and becoming a doctor. She knew she didn't want to live as her mother had. Her teachers had said she was smart and could do anything, but she wasn't so sure. "I don't know if I can refuse him," she mumbled to her sister.

"I know how you feel, Kerri," Amanda whispered. "It's hard to hold back when you think you're in love. James and I thought we were in love. We'd gone together for two whole years before we decided to go all the way. I really thought I knew him, but after we started having sex it seemed like we weren't as close as we were before."

Kerri frowned. "I don't understand."

"It was like sex became our only reason for getting together. We didn't talk anymore like we had before. To tell the truth, there were times when I just wanted to be held, but he seemed to feel we had to do it every time."

"But isn't it just the most fantastic feeling in the world ... I mean the movies make it look—"

"Movies aren't reality, Kerri!" Amanda focused her heavily lashed eyes on her younger sister. "The first time was painful and awkward, and afterward I felt horribly guilty. I never did experience the fireworks like you see in the movies."

Kerri looked at her sister sympathetically. "Why did James leave when you got pregnant?"

"He couldn't handle it. He wasn't ready to be a father. Of course I wasn't ready to be a mother either, but I couldn't stand the thought of an abortion. We talked just before he left. We both decided that we'd made a terrible mistake when we changed our relationship to a sexual one. Before that we were like best friends. We enjoyed being together, having fun, and being carefree. I wish it could be like that again," she finished softly.

Kerri thought of what her sister had said for a long time. She thought of the sad look in her sister's eyes and the unhappy tone in her voice. Would it be like that for her, or was Ben different? She was sure he loved her, and she didn't want to risk losing that love. She knew she had to give him an answer soon.

Kerri is like millions of girls who are looking for love and think that having sex is the way to get it. Look at the large number of single teenage mothers and ask yourself if Kerri is right. Talk with several teenage mothers and find out if things have turned out the way they had thought they would. Some of these young mothers will tell you that they were not terribly upset when the father of their baby left because by that time they had discovered that they didn't love him anyway.

Eighteen-year-old Chanda admitted to me that she was glad her child's father was out of her life. "I was looking forward to being a mother," Chanda told me as she pushed her wavy blond hair away from her face. "The thought of having my own little baby to care for was exciting. I'd never felt much love from my family, but now I'd have my own child to love and to love me back."

"How is it, now that Robby is two?" I ask her.

"It's hard . . . really hard," she said. "I have to get up at five o'clock every morning, and get him ready to go to the babysitter's. I go to school until one, then straight to work until seven and back to pick him up at the sitter's. I have no social life and very little fun." She lowered her pale blue eyes and watched as Robby played with a toy. "I wasn't ready to be a mother," she whispered. "I know that now."

There are thousands of babies being born to unwed teenage mothers every year. Many of these girls thought, as Chanda did, that it would be fun to have their own baby. What they couldn't imagine, however, is the tremendous responsibility that goes along with raising a child. The more mature we are, the more financially secure, and the more life experience we have behind us, the more ready we are to be mothers or fathers and the better our parenting will be. Every child born is precious and deserves to have not only the best mothering possible but also the best fathering. If every child born had loving, nurturing, self-disciplined parents who provided guidance and intelligent discipline, our social problems would be practically nonexistent.

Pregnancy is only one of the severe consequences that can result from having sex too soon. A moment of sexual irresponsibility can leave a person with a sexually transmitted disease that will last a lifetime. There are more than twenty sexually transmitted diseases. *Planned Parenthood's Guide to Sexual Health* lists and discusses fourteen of the more common ones. Seven of these diseases are so serious a health threat they must be reported to local public health departments. None of the sexually transmitted diseases are trivial. They range from recurring outbreaks of the herpes simplex II virus, which causes uncomfortable, painful sores and blisters in the genital area, to full-blown cases of AIDS, which is fatal. Both are incurable. Gonorrhea is an extremely contagious disease and can spread throughout the body, causing serious problems. It is especially dangerous because it can spread without noticeable symptoms until it is too late. In women it can result in permanent sterility. Syphilis, though less common, can result in damage to the brain and nervous system. It can be cured, but any damage done to the brain cannot be reversed.

Most public schools now offer educational programs describing each disease and its effects on the body. If your school does not offer such a program, it would be smart to talk with your parents about this subject, and to get information at the library, Planned Parenthood, or any other clinic that offers sex-education materials. Become informed. Studies have shown that teens who know the facts about sex are more likely to act responsibly and control their sexual feeling until they know the time is right. With the rise of AIDS, I believe that teenagers would be wise to postpone sex until they have completed their education and know in their hearts they are ready for a committed, monogamous, mature relationship. Remember, the best way for teenagers to avoid unwanted pregnancy and sexually transmitted diseases is to wait until marriage for a sexually intimate relationship.

If, after deep thought and consideration, you feel you must enter into a sexual relationship, it is imperative that you do so wisely. Couples may fall into bed spontaneously in the movies, but in real life it is something that should be discussed with your partner first. You should know about your partner's sexual history. Make an appointment at a family planning clinic and get information on birth control and safe sex. Entering into a sexual relationship without doing these things would be like driving down the freeway blindfolded. Know where you're going and plan the way intelligently.

Sex is like a gift that God has given us. The gift comes with a note that says we can open the gift when we know the time is right for us. There is also a warning that we must use the gift well, care for it, protect it, and share it judiciously. There is also a promise that if we do all these things, the gift will enhance our spirituality. As we receive the gift, the gratitude in our heart mingles with

the knowledge that whenever there is a positive, a negative is possible, too. Just as right use can enhance our
spirituality, wrong use can wound it.

PRIDE

If you look up the word "pride" in the dictionary you
can get confused. First it says, "inordinate self-esteem,
conceit," and next it says, "a reasonable or justifiable
self-respect." It does seem strange, but just as with everything else in life, something good, when carried to an
extreme, can be bad. No one would disagree that
healthy self-esteem is beneficial to a person's well-being.
The problem occurs when we let our pride overshadow
our common sense and our freedom to love.

When I was fourteen, my friend Karen and I rode
our bicycles to the community swimming pool six blocks
from home. It was mid-January and extremely cold in
the Colorado town where I lived. The pool was closed
for the season but was still filled with water—icy water.
We got off our bikes and walked to the edge of the pool.
Swimming had always been one of my favorite activities,
and I thought I was an excellent swimmer. "I'd like to
dive in and swim across the pool," I declared.

Karen laughed. "You couldn't possibly make it across
in that cold water."

"Sure I could," I said, confident in my swimming ability.

"I dare you, then!" she challenged.

"What'll you give me if I do?"

"If you make it across the width of the pool, I'll give
you twenty dollars." Her mocking voice made it clear
that she didn't think I'd do it. I knew I could do it, and
it would serve her right to lose twenty dollars.

"You're on!" I shouted. We were standing by the deep end of the pool, and I was ready to jump in when she urged me to go down to the shallow end. I was perfectly confident, but something made me agree to her suggestion. I marched toward the other end, peeling off my heavy jacket. I pulled off my sneakers and, in my jeans and sweatshirt, jumped in the icy water and started swimming as fast as I could. I made it about two-thirds of the way when my will, my courage, and my pride were all depleted. The water was colder than I'd ever imagined. I staggered to my feet and dragged myself from the pool. Karen was aghast at what I'd done. "Bonnie, you must be crazy!" she blurted as she grabbed my jacket and helped me into it. I was never so cold in all my life as I pedaled the six blocks to my house. Thank goodness my mother wasn't home to find out what I'd done. Karen was worried I'd get pneumonia. She made tea while I changed clothes. As I sat in the kitchen gulping the hot tea, I knew what I'd done was stupid. If I'd jumped in the deep end, as I was about to, I could have drowned. Luckily I didn't get pneumonia; neither did I get the twenty dollars. What I did get was a lesson in humility and the folly of too much pride.

The single greatest thing that causes us to forget good judgment and do or say dumb things is too much pride. Pride can break up friendships, rip families apart, and cause fights between individuals and groups, as well as wars between nations. Pride is like poison to our spiritual growth. Pride can block our openness and our ability to learn new things. It can mar the way we adapt to change and accept new ideas. People who take such excessive pride in their religion, their nationality, or their race that they lose their objectivity may be creating barriers between themselves and others who are different.

To retain self-esteem while letting go of pride is tricky, but it can be done. Through love it is possible. If we love ourselves enough, we don't need pride to deal with life. Through love we are able to accept other people who are different from us. We can allow them their beliefs without feeling threatened. Only when we reach the point where we can accept others the way they are, letting them have their own beliefs, their own way of doing things, can we ever expect to have any real peace in the world. If what others are doing is not harming anyone, then we must learn to allow them the freedom to do their thing.

FEAR OF FAILURE

A very significant thing that holds teens back from achieving their dreams is the fear of failure. As I indicated earlier, I took drama when I was a senior in high school. I loved performing. I loved being someone else for a while and exploring different characters. Everything about the theater excited me. But when it came time to choose what to do with my life, I decided that aspiring to be an actress was too lofty a goal. There was so much competition that I'd probably never make it anyway. So I chose to teach drama instead of pursuing an acting career. I have found other avenues for self-expression, but there will always be a part of me that will wonder, "What if?"

We must strive to do what we love doing or our lives will be tainted with regret. If we will put our total focus on our dream and refuse to give in to the fear that we may not make it, our chances of succeeding are very great. It doesn't mean it will come easy or that we won't make mistakes along the way. The important thing to recognize is that value lies in the journey toward our dreams as much as in the final destination. If we drop our fears, ignore our self-created limitations, and go for our dreams, our hearts will be fulfilled. It really doesn't matter how much money we make or how much we accomplish as long as we're doing what we enjoy.

The more pitfalls and mistakes we can avoid on our journey through life, the more energy we can devote to fulfilling our dreams. We will make mistakes, however, and when we do we must admit the mistake. Only by admitting it can we learn the lesson our mistake teaches us. It is in the lessons learned from our mistakes that we are able to grow spiritually.

CHAPTER V

Relating to Parents

Our relationship with our parents goes through many stages, but the most difficult stage is reached when we enter puberty. Teenagers struggle with the conflict of being dependent on their parents and, at the same time, wanting to establish their independence. Many times the conflicts that arise out of this struggle cause resentments that hurt the relationship we have with our parents. Sometimes the conflicts become so severe that the home becomes a battleground and our parents the enemy.

We can save ourselves and our parents a lot of unhappiness if we will take time to understand them and find out how they got to be the way they are. We have to see more than what is happening at the present moment. Parents are products of their past experiences, as we all are. We can ask what life was like for them when they were growing up. We can try to understand the problems and fears they faced as children. We may begin to see that their attitudes come from their own parents, the society in which they grew up, and the ideas they've adopted about how to be a good parent. They may seem unenlightened to us, or hopelessly old-fashioned, or just plain wrong, but instead of wishing they'd change, we can choose to accept them as they are. We must realize they are doing the best they can, given their stage of spiritual awareness. What more can we expect?

Parents want their sons and daughters to be happy. Many times, however, they don't have the skills needed for parenting and so their relationship with their children becomes a struggle. Born of the struggle are resentment, misunderstanding, anger, and imprudent reactions. Parents sometimes say very cruel things to their children in an attempt to change their behavior. Nearly always the cruel things are said impulsively, without thought or even awareness of the hurt that they inflict on the teenager. What we must try to understand is that when parents say cruel things, they often do not realize what they are doing. Frustration, anger, and fear are the cause of their cruelty. The parent who has not learned parenting skills is at a loss in knowing how to deal with these feelings. So the parent will mimic the reactions of their own parents in similar situations. Their parents, of course, were equally unskilled at raising children, just as their parents were before them.

TRY UNCONDITIONAL LOVE

How does a teenager deal with reactionary parents—parents who scream and yell and seem to lack love? You might begin by giving your parents the thing that you want from them: unconditional love. You want them to love you no matter what, but are you willing to do this for your parents? Are you willing to love them despite their flaws, their attitudes, and their behavior, dropping your judgments of them and accepting them just as they are? Loving your parents unconditionally is a freeing experience. When you are no longer judging them and wanting them to be different, when you give up the idea that they could do better if they wanted to, you will find yourself more relaxed around them. Now you are free to discover what you like about them because you're no longer dwelling on what you don't like.

In asking for this kind of openness and understanding toward your parents, I realize how difficult it is. Many situations require that teenagers act with greater wisdom than their own parents possess. I also realize that the traditional patterns of argument—a parent's dominance and a child's resistance—are enormously difficult to overcome. But lashing out accomplishes nothing, and the process of striving for calm, open discussion, however difficult it may be, is everybody's best hope for a happy and successful home life.

When we choose to love our parents unconditionally, we make a conscious decision to love them regardless of how they act. This doesn't mean we have to approve of how they behave or agree with their opinions. It doesn't mean we should condone their cruelty (if that is a problem). It simply means we decide to reach out to them with understanding and compassion rather than withdrawing, as our ego would dictate. By reaching out we are giving our parents the unconditional love their own parents never gave them. In doing this we nurture our own and our parents' spiritual nature.

UNDERSTANDING YOUR PARENTS

There are two major things teens can do to improve their relationship with their parents. First, when a parent is angry and is coming down on the teenager, the teen can try to understand where his parent's anger is coming from. Let's say you're running around with some kids your parents don't like. Try to see the situation from their point of view. They may be afraid these friends will lead you to some kind of harm. They may fear these new friends will destroy the values they have tried to instill in you. Since they don't really know these kids they will judge them on what they see—their clothes, their behavior, etc. Perhaps you could try to see them as your parents do. Ask yourself if your parents could possibly be right about them. Realize that Mom and Dad aren't objecting to them in order to destroy your fun, but because they are genuinely concerned about you.

If, after thoughtful contemplation, you are sure that your parents' worries are unfounded, help your parents to get to know your friend as you do. You could say, "Mom, Dad, I know that Sherry dresses kind of different, but she really has a good heart." Talk about Sherry's character qualities. Give them some examples that will help them to know her as a person. If you help your parents see beyond the image, their fears will dissolve and they will accept your new friend.

Perhaps your mom is angry because you lost your car keys. Trace her anger and you may find that she is worried that you are undisciplined or irresponsible. This reflects on her and the image she has of herself as a "good" mother. Your dad yells at you because your grades have fallen on your report card. Look past the anger and you could see that he is afraid that you may not graduate, may not get into college, or in general may not make it in life—a multitude of fears could be behind his anger. The thing to remember is that the fears would not be there if he didn't care about you. It's not that parents don't love their teens, it's that they have not learned how to communicate their concerns. They are ruled by fear, and fear is very uncomfortable. Parents hate to feel it, and when the teen causes the parent to feel its cold grip, the parent reacts with anger.

COMMUNICATING WITH PARENTS

The second thing teens can do to help improve their relationship with parents is to learn to communicate better. During a calm moment ask your parents if you can talk. Let them know your feelings about things. If they try to tell you that you shouldn't feel that way, insist (in a calm way) that to try not to feel something you do feel is dishonest, and that you want to be as open and honest with them as possible. This can be the beginning of a new and better relationship with your parents. The book *Making Peace with Your Parents,* by Harold Bloomfield, gives some constructive advice on communicating with your parents. Dr. Bloomfield asserts that until we let go of our resentments toward our parents and love them unconditionally, we will not be free to experience the joy and fulfillment that life has to offer.

BEING RECEPTIVE

Parents want to be listened to in an open way. Many teens are so sure that their parents have nothing to say—nothing they haven't heard before, anyway—that they shut out their parents' words. We shut our parents out by becoming defensive. We are so busy devising our defenses that we don't hear them. We expect things to go badly, and we generally get what we expect. We consider ourselves victims and don't even consider the possibility of taking responsibility for bettering the relationship.

There have been times when I've felt extremely frustrated with my teenagers. Recently we have been having a problem with our thirteen-year-old twins being ready for school on time in the mornings. I called for a family conference about the matter.

"I'm unhappy with the recent situation we've been experiencing in the mornings," I began. I noticed that one of the girls was sitting with her arms crossed and her eyes turned away from me. It irritated me, but I continued calmly. "When you don't give yourself enough time to get ready in the morning, you become stressed, then any little thing sets off your anger and the whole family begins to feel the effect." The other girl was sitting in an open body position and had her eyes on me while I was speaking. It made me feel that she was receptive and open to modifying her behavior. Her sister, however, maintained her previous position. I felt she was being resistant and hostile. "Will you please uncross your arms and look at me when I'm speaking," I said, feeling my irritation growing.

She glared at me. "Why should I?" she muttered.

"Because I need to feel you're hearing me and that you're open to what I'm saying. You girls have a problem, and it's causing a problem for our whole family. I want to see you're willing to find a solution." I understood that her position was simply a defense against what she perceived as personal criticism, but that didn't make it any less frustrating.

Teenagers will find more peace and harmony in their relationship with their parents if they will drop their

defenses and be open with them. It's this defensive pos-
ture that always gets us in trouble. We don't need to
defend ourselves from everything that's said or done to
us. We can choose to be open and receptive without
sacrificing anything. It's when we let ourselves get torn
apart with anger and resentment that we lose pieces of
ourselves. To be whole is to broaden our vision so it
includes more than self at the center of everything. Being open doesn't mean you have to agree with your
parents, just listen in an open way. By using understanding we can rid ourselves of anger, and we won't
need defenses. When we listen in a receptive way, our
parents are likely to listen to our feelings and opinions,
and communication grows.

James is an only child. His parents expect a great deal
from him. He is expected to get good grades and to get
into Harvard Law School. In short, he is expected to
become a success. James feels overwhelmed with all the
expectations his parents put on him. He needs to reduce
the pressure, and the only way he can do this is to say
something like, "Mom and Dad, I know you love me,
and I know you want me to have a successful and happy
life. I want very much for you to be proud of me. Your
love and respect means a great deal to me. I have some
concerns that I'd like to share with you, and I need you
to listen to what I have to say before responding."

By starting the conversation with the assurances of
the love that they have for each other, James is creating
an atmosphere in which his parents will be more receptive to what he has to say. Now he must share his feelings honestly and unwaveringly, making sure to remain
calm and cool all the while. Afterward he must listen
openly to what his parents have to say, without arguing,

either verbally or in his mind. By sharing his feelings in
this way, James helps create understanding and closeness with his parents.

ACKNOWLEDGING PARENTS' FEELINGS

Teens can easily avoid confrontations with their parents. Instead of meeting their opinions and comments
with a battering-ram attitude, acknowledge their feelings by showing that you understand what they are saying. Sometimes it's appropriate to give your opinion and
sometimes it's not. If you wish to disagree with your
parents, do it diplomatically. You can say something
like, "I see what you mean, but have you ever thought of
this . . . ?"

Parents don't want confrontations with their teenagers. What they want is that their children recognize
their complaints. If teens will respond to parents' complaints with a simple sentence of recognition and acceptance, rather than resistance, the home will be much
more peaceful. Parents and teenagers alike will be
happier.

BUILDING TRUST

Parents want to trust their children, but their trust seems
to diminish as their kids get older. One reason for this
is the increased freedom that teens have and the dwin-
dling control the parents have over the teen. Parents
may remember the things they used to do when they
were young, and they want to protect their kids from
the mistakes they made. Parents are also afraid of the

increased dangers in our modern world, such as drugs, alcohol, venereal disease, and AIDS.

One way teens can maximize the trust that parents show them is by never doing anything that would give their parents reason not to trust them. If you say you will be home by ten o'clock, be there by ten. If there is some reason why you can't possibly make it by ten, always call and let them know. If you say you'll do something, whether it's take out the trash or care for a pet, do it, and do it on schedule. If for some reason you slip up, be honest and let your parents know. They may be upset at first, but they will respect your honesty and understand that you value their trust.

If parents can be sure you will always do your best to do as you say you will, they will trust you. They will relax their control and give you more freedom. Trust is earned and, once earned, is much easier to preserve than it is to regain, if it's lost.

ACCEPTING VALUE JUDGMENTS

Beginning in childhood, we start to compile a list of rights and wrongs, goods and bads in our minds. The items on our list become our value judgments. If one of your mother's value judgments is that good people make their beds first thing every morning, then you can understand why it bothers her that you don't make your bed in the morning. You are her child. Her expectation is that you are a good person, so it drives her up a wall when you don't make your bed.

By the time kids have reached their teenage years they, too, have formed many value judgments. When Cory's mom took a job as a barmaid in a local tavern,

Cory was outraged. He just couldn't accept the fact that his mom worked in a bar. He had a preconceived idea of barmaids as being uneducated, sleazy, and of low moral character, and he was furious that his mom would choose such a job. Cory's relationship with his mom deteriorated and the atmosphere in their home became volcanic.

If we and our parents could drop our value judgments, and stop looking at everything as good or bad, right or wrong, we could be more open to each other, more accepting of each other's differences, attitudes, and lifestyles. This is not likely to happen, however, so the next best thing is for us to be aware of our parents' value judgments and accept them. This helps us to understand ourselves and our parents better. When we understand that it's our ideas of good and bad, right and wrong, that cause our conflicts, we are freed from the hurt of disappointment and disapproval.

LEARN TO COMPROMISE

It was a warm Sunday morning and Pam didn't feel like going to church with her family, but she knew they were expecting her presence, so she reluctantly began getting ready. She looked in her closet for something to wear and spotted the new, cropped shirt she'd bought at the mall the day before. She quickly slipped it on, along with her short skirt and sandals, and headed out the door.

"You're not wearing that halter top to church," her mother told her.

Pam shot a defiant glare at her mom. "It's not a halter top," she said flatly.

"It leaves your midriff bare, and I'd call it a halter top," her mom insisted.

Pam grimaced. Why was her mother so old-fashioned? "Everybody wears tops like this," she insisted.

"I don't care what everybody wears. That's inappropriate for church. Now go change," her mother ordered.

"If I can't wear this, I'm not going to church!" Pam exploded as she dashed for her room.

Many times mothers and daughters get into a power struggle over what looks good and what doesn't. Daughters think their moms are old-fashioned and uninformed about what's in. Mothers think their daughters are dressing inappropriately or provocatively. What mothers and daughters need to understand is that their value judgments are tied to their views about wearing apparel.

While society has become more flexible about what is considered fashionable, many moms are looking at fashion with a viewpoint originating two decades earlier. Teens need to understand that moms can't entirely control that. Pam and her mother need to learn to compromise about the clothes she wears. Mothers can learn to let up on trying to control everything their teenage daughters buy and wear, and teens can show a willingness to listen to their mothers' opinions.

We form many of our tastes and opinions in our teenage years, and it is only natural that as we become more confident in ourselves, we become more assertive. Parents may understand this and accept that their teenagers will be likely to disagree with them on certain issues. But if teens and parents each refuse to acknowledge the other's point of view, these issues can escalate into serious disagreements. The only real solution to difficult problems between young people and their parents is compromise, and compromise begins with communication.

LET GO OF THE NEED TO BE RIGHT

Have you ever known someone who always had to be right? Perhaps you've noticed this tendency in yourself or you've seen it in a friend. Maybe one of your parents is this way. You may get angry when dealing with someone who's like this. You may see them as arrogant or stubborn. We must understand, however, that the need to be right is born out of insecurity.

We don't always have to be right. We don't always have to get in the last word. Instead of letting yourself get involved in a power struggle with someone over who is right and who is wrong, give yourself time for some rigorous self-examination. If, after some time in thoughtful contemplation, you still feel you are right, choose a time when everyone is calm and discuss the issue rationally. Don't label the other person as wrong; just concentrate on how you feel and why.

Danielle's father made a statement at the dinner table that interracial marriage was wrong. Danielle disagreed with him, and they became embroiled in a discussion that became more and more heated as time went on. What Danielle and her father needed to realize was that it is okay to disagree, that one of them doesn't have to be right and the other wrong. They must learn to respect each other's opinions and give each other the right to feel differently.

What if Danielle's father refuses to respect her opinion, however, and insists that she agree that he is right? In a case like this it is pointless for Danielle to continue the argument. She can say something like, "I can understand why you feel the way you do, Dad. I'll think about what you've said, and I'd like you to think about my views, too. We don't have to agree on this in order to love each other." Then she could kiss her father on the cheek or give him a hug, and the situation is defused. By doing this Danielle creates peace in the family without becoming a victim.

Some of my most vivid memories of my childhood were of my older sister and my father arguing. They were both assertive and very strong-willed. As a child twelve years younger than my sister, I didn't understand what all the quarreling was about, but it upset me. I made up my mind at a very young age that I was going to have a better relationship with my father than my sister had. I learned how to communicate with him so he didn't become angry. I learned to listen to his point of view and to think before I spoke. I remember once when I was sixteen my boyfriend bought me a pearl ring. "I want you to give the ring back," my dad said.

I was perplexed. "Why?" I asked.

"Because if you keep it, he will think you've agreed to marry him." I didn't think my father was right, but I knew he was worried I might marry too young. What would it hurt if I gave the ring back. I knew I could make my boyfriend understand. It wouldn't cause a serious problem between us, so I agreed to give back the ring. I didn't know it at the time, but I had learned to bend my will in order to achieve a greater good, which was my relationship with my father. Because I was willing to bend, we had a very close and loving relationship, and I don't feel I sacrificed anything.

LET GO OF THE NEED TO BLAME

Blame is a good ego defense. We use blame to protect ourselves from having to take responsibility for our own lives. When we blame others for things going wrong in our lives, we build resentment within our own heart. We see ourselves as victims and surrender responsibility for our own happiness to others.

Doug blamed his mother for his parents' divorce. His father had been a workaholic, spending little time at home and focusing nearly all his attention on his job. After twelve years of this, Doug's mom asked for a divorce. Doug was devastated. He had seen little enough of his father before the divorce. Now he saw him even less. Doug thought his mom should have been more understanding and less demanding with his father. He hated her for how she had nagged his father before the divorce. Doug thought she had only considered herself and hadn't taken into account his needs. So now his father was gone and he blamed his mom.

As long as Doug holds on to his need to blame his mom, there is not much hope for their relationship. Doug will feel resentment, anger, and distrust toward his mother. If Doug can stop blaming his mom, and see the divorce for what it is—two people agreeing not to live together anymore—he will free himself from all these negative emotions. Then instead of using his energy to blame his mother, he can use it to establish a closer relationship with his father. Letting go of blame is necessary if we are to make spiritual progress.

UNDERSTANDING THE NEED FOR APPROVAL

Our need for approval from our parents creates stress in our relationship with them. This resulting stress is the thing that blocks our ability to love unconditionally. In *Making Peace with Your Parents,* Harold Bloomfield writes that this approval trap ties us to wishing our parents were different, resenting that they aren't, resisting their advice, feeling trapped by their expectations, feeling driven to defy or conform to their values, and feeling defensive and unloving when we are with them.

The need for approval from our parents lies deep within our being. Some of us try to deny this need by living our lives in resistance to our parents, by rejecting their values and advice. Others bury their own desires and needs in order to please Mom and Dad. Neither way offers a very satisfactory solution to peaceful coexistence. The first way, living in resistance, results in outward fighting and explosive disagreements. The second way, giving in to gain parental approval, results in inward anger, resentment, and frustration. Everything may appear calm on the surface, but the teen feels that he's hiding his true self from his parents. He feels they don't really know him at all.

So what is the solution to the approval trap? First, we must recognize our own inner need for our parents' approval. Second, we must establish the most honest relationship with our parents that is possible, given their degree of openness or rigidness. Third, we must realize that there are times when we must bend. Our relationship with our parents is one of the most important relationships we will have in life, and it is to our advantage to nurture that relationship. To bend is to comply or yield to our parents' values and opinions when those values or opinions are not in direct opposition to the way we feel. We must learn to bend but not to break. When a parent makes demands on a child that are in direct opposition to his own inner nature, then that child, no matter what age, must let go of his need for parental approval and calmly but firmly resist.

It's a sad fact, but there are some parents who try to force their kids to do things that are illegal, immoral, or dangerous. When this happens, the child feels deep within that there is something not right about this. He feels uneasy and confused. He is torn between wanting to please his parent and not wanting to do whatever the parent is trying to get him to do. To give in to a parent's demands, when that small voice deep inside is crying "no," is to hurt ourselves spiritually. We must be true to ourselves first and resist when our inner voice warns us that something isn't right.

Most parents, however, are motivated by wanting what is best or what they think is best for their child. Sam loved sports and working with kids, but from the time he was small, his father had dreamed of him becoming a doctor and joining his own successful practice. His father had spoken so often of Sam becoming a doctor that it was just understood and accepted by the whole family that Sam would fulfill his father's dream. The trouble was that it wasn't Sam's dream. Sam knew down deep that he wanted to be a coach and work with young kids, but he loved his father and he didn't want to disappoint him. He couldn't bring himself to be honest with his father about what he really wanted to do with his life. When a person acquiesces, submitting to his parents' wishes rather than listening to his own heart, he is no longer bending. He is breaking spiritually, and this is sad indeed.

If we could simply sit down with our parents and agree that we don't have to conform to each other's ideas of the perfect parent or the perfect child, and if we could agree to accept each other for the individuals that we happen to be, we could save ourselves a great deal of pain and unhappiness. If we could agree to stop playing the old approval game and just love each other, we could improve our relationship with our parents, and they could improve their relationship with us. There are no guarantees in life, but it seems to me that it's worth a try.

DEALING WITH AN ABUSIVE PARENT

Some families are controlled by angry, hostile, cruel, spiritually ill people. A parent like this, one who is addicted to alcohol, or drugs, one who inflicts sexual abuse, physical abuse, or severe mental abuse, is an individual who is spiritually retarded. Kids who grow up in homes with such a parent may deal all their life with the shame, the suppressed rage, and the spiritual hurt they suffered while growing up. Mom and Dad are supposed to provide security, not pain, and it is not unusual for young people to blame themselves for the abuse heaped on them by their parents. Professional help is generally required in order for these adolescents to achieve healing from their wounds.

The first thing a teenager must realize is that what has happened to him is not his fault. He must recognize the burden of guilt and shame he has been carrying around, and he must be willing to seek help to release this bur-

den. Teachers, counselors, pastors, and, in some communities, teenage crisis hot lines are good sources of
help. Some teens have complained that when they
sought help, someone didn't believe them. If this happens the teen must not give up. He must keep looking
until he finds someone who is willing to listen.

How does a teenager who has been severely abused
reconcile to the fact that his parent, who is supposed to
love him, has in truth abused him? This situation can be
dealt with through an understanding of paradox. A paradox is an idea that seems to be false but may be true.
It's something that at first doesn't make sense. The statement "He that loseth his life . . . shall find it" is a paradox.

The only way to reconcile severe abuse is by accepting
the paradox that freedom comes, not through revenge,
but through forgiveness. An abused teenager can recognize that, though he had no choice in the abuse he
suffered, he does have a choice in how he will react to
that abuse. Peace of mind can be found when the teenager sees what his parent has done to him, acknowl-
edges the abuse, and then consciously chooses to release
the hurt, the anger, and the blame.

Many times the teen uses anger to protect himself
from the hurt he doesn't want to feel. In this way he
hides his pain from himself. To be free, he must let go
of his anger and allow the hurt to surface. This can be
very difficult, but in order to come to terms with the
abuse the teenager must see and feel the pain he has
suffered. With courage, he must confront the pain until
his spirit reacts and tears roll freely down his cheeks. At
that point he will notice a swell of compassion for the
hurt child within him that is being revealed. Now he can

forgive himself for the bad feelings he has had for his parent, for underneath these bad feelings and thoughts is a lot of guilt that needs to be released.

At this point the teenager is ready to forgive his parent. One way he might do this is by going into a meditative, prayerful state and asking his higher self, his self that is greater than his ego, to help him forgive the parent who abused him. In cases of extreme abuse, forgiveness may seem impossible, but our higher self knows that until we forgive we can never be free. Anger, resentment, and the need for revenge chain us to the person who abused us. Until we can look him in the eyes, and choose understanding rather than revenge, compassion rather than anger, love rather than hate, we will not free ourselves from those chains. Until we are free we cannot progress spiritually. The key is choosing to forgive—not for our parent, but for ourself. It is done out of our own choice and our own power. Once we make the choice we can ask God to help us release our negative emotions. We can say silently, "I recognize that my parent has wronged me. I choose to leave his (her) judgment to God. With God's help I am releasing all the bad things I've felt toward my parent. I choose to do this because I want to be free. I want peace, harmony, and love to fill my being. I know that God within me will make it so."

Many times we are reluctant to forgive because the need for revenge is so strong. Look at it this way. You wouldn't hate someone who was mentally retarded or physically deformed, even if that person's affliction impacted your life negatively. Instead you would excuse their afflictions and feel compassion for them. Likewise, we must see that some people are spiritual cripples.

They have chosen to think negatively and act negatively. They have let anger, resentment, fear, insecurity, and ill will rob them of peace, harmony, love, and well-being. It is for our own peace of mind that we must drop our resentments and anger toward them and let go of our desire to blame them. We must recognize that if we don't think of them with compassion, we will become just like them. So we choose to forgive, for our own peace and well-being, and so that we can be free of the hurt and pain they have caused us. It is like a cut on your finger. You remember it months later, but it doesn't hurt anymore because it has healed. When you forgive with compassion, your spiritual hurt is healed and you are free.

This is only a brief explanation of the process involved in forgiveness. Entire books have been written on this subject, and the teenager who has been severely abused may be able to find solace in them. On the other hand, he may need to seek professional help in order to free himself from the pain of his abuse. Whatever path toward healing he chooses, he must understand that many years of anger and suppressed pain are not healed in a day. Perseverance and the willingness to put in the work necessary, however, will lead to health, harmony, and peace of mind.

CHAPTER VI

Right Thinking

There are two kinds of thinking: disciplined thinking and undisciplined thinking. Undisciplined thinking is the kind used by most people in our world, people who are not conscious or aware of how our thinking impacts our lives. Thoughts pop into our heads and we follow them like a kitten after a string. Sometimes these thoughts lead us into great trouble and cause great problems in our lives, but we seldom make the connection between the way we think and these problems.

When Neil was in second grade, he was out sick for a week. When he came back to school the teacher was talking about borrowing in subtraction. He was confused and upset that he didn't understand it. Doubt about his intelligence crept into his mind. He began thinking thoughts like, *I'm dumb, I'll never understand, I can't do math, I hate math.* The more he thought like this, the worse he got at math. This is how we are. We have an experience and from that experience we form a belief. Once we believe something subconsciously, we expect it to be true, and before very long we find it is true.

I like to think of my subconscious as my own unique computer inside my mind. My computer can be programmed only by me. The thoughts, attitudes, and beliefs that I program into my computer create the story of my life. If I want my story to be happy, to include love, success, and abundance, then these are the kinds of thoughts I must program into my computer. If I find things in my life I don't like, such as fear, anger, failure, or poverty, I recognize that I am the one responsible for the negative thought programming that brought these conditions into my life. If I don't like the story my computer is printing out, I can choose to change the story by deleting my negative programming. I do this by finding and letting go of old destructive beliefs. Then I reprogram with positive, affirmative thoughts that become new beliefs that create my revised life story.

Most of us let our experiences create our beliefs, and then we wonder why our lives are not going well. When we awaken to how our subconscious takes these beliefs and creates our reality, we will begin to consciously choose our beliefs through a process of right thinking. When this occurs, we awaken to our unlimited potential. Disciplined thinking means we take charge of our own mind and choose to think only constructive, loving, positive, creative kinds of thoughts. When negative, destructive thoughts enter our minds, we acknowledge them, understand they come from our hurts, fears, anger, etc., and then consciously let them go. After a while these kinds of thoughts will enter our mind less and less, and in time we will become true masters of our own destiny.

Look around at the older people you know. Notice the ones who have a positive outlook on life, who always see the good in others, who never complain or blame others. Notice the kind of reality they've created for themselves. Usually they are people who are enjoying life. They are involved, caring, fun people to be around.

Now notice those older individuals who are always

talking about how bad things are, people who don't trust anyone, who are always blaming others for the bad things in their lives, and notice what their life is like. Usually the first thing you will notice is that they are not physically well individuals. They talk a great deal about their illnesses. Their finances are in bad shape or they think they are. Some may have a lot of money, but they have a poverty attitude so they don't enjoy it, share it, or use it beneficially. Their relationships are generally not working well. They don't seem to enjoy life and are always complaining. Is it just that life (or God) has been unfair to them, or could they be reaping the effects of a lifetime of negative thinking?

Negative, destructive thoughts tear down rather than support or build up. They create a pessimistic attitude that colors everything that happens. If we fill our minds with bad thoughts it's like filling our stomachs with bad food. It will block our feelings of well-being. Whenever we think a negative thought, it's like adding a brick to a gunnysack that we must carry around on our back. Too many negative thoughts will pull us down emotionally and spiritually.

I was in my forties before I learned how to think. Before that many of my thoughts were motivated by fear, limitation, and frustration. If my checkbook didn't balance, I'd think, *I am awful at math.* If my dinner burned, *I'm a terrible cook.* When I learned that the words "I am" have power and should be used cautiously, I began to discipline my thinking.

Never think, *I can't do that, I'm not smart enough, I'm not pretty, or strong, or healthy, or organized,* or any other limiting thought. If you don't believe in yourself, how can you expect anyone else to? Always believe in you and you'll be surprised at what you can do. For we become what we think we are. No one ever did anything until they first thought they could do it. If we always expect the best, the best will eventually express itself in our lives.

BE A FREE THINKER

Our thoughts are never really our own unless we become conscious of how our parents, our peers, and society in general have molded our thinking. We must learn to sift through the ideas that have been impressed upon us and decide for ourselves what we believe.

The enormous influence of the advertising business in America is a good illustration of how powerful thoughts are. The advertisers aren't selling products, they are actually selling beliefs. It's the belief that makes us go out and buy the product. If they can get us to believe that a certain aspirin is more effective, we will buy it. If they can make us believe we will be more successful if we dress a certain way, more sexy if we wear a certain perfume, or more popular if we serve a certain kind of beverage at a party, we will purchase their product. During the late fall and winter months, we are bombarded by ads telling us that flu season is here and sounding as though getting the flu was inevitable. Do you suppose believing that message might have an impact on whether we get sick or not?

The society in which we grow up has a great influence on what we believe and how we think. In hundreds of different ways society tells us what to believe. If we grow up in a rigidly religious atmosphere, we will think differently than if we grow up in a more free, open atmosphere. Most of our beliefs are formed when we are very young and influence the way we think about everything. Our thinking grows out of our limited experience; therefore, our perspective—the way we see life—is limited. The good news is, however, that we are conscious beings and are able to consciously let go of old, destructive beliefs. We can choose to base our beliefs on something larger than ourselves—the sum total of all that is good in the universe. There is always more than one way to look at things. We can choose to look at things positively rather than negatively. We can focus on the good in the world, and observe the great strides man is making in science, medicine, the environment, etc., or we can view everything as an overwhelming problem. We can think of our world as about to die from pollution, deforestation, and oil spills, or we can focus on the great things being done to solve these problems. We aren't talking about living in illusion but focusing on the good that is available to us rather than dwelling on the bad.

My nephew, Andy, is a passionate environmentalist. When my eldest daughter was in her midteens, he stayed with us for a while. He liked to share his consuming interest in the environment, and she was a good listener, so he'd talk to her for hours. One day, after noticing how his total focus was on the destruction of the planet, I took him aside.

"I don't want you talking with Kim anymore about the environment," I said.

He looked startled. "Why not?"

"Because you don't present a balanced view. You only tell the negative side, and you paint a terribly grim picture."

"The situation is grim," he said. "I think teenagers need to know what's happening to their planet."

"But when you talk only of the destruction, and share with her your bitterness toward humanity for causing it, you're scaring her and leaving her with the idea that things are hopeless."

"Things are hopeless," he muttered.

Irritation slithered up my spine. "That's your opinion, Andy, and I won't have you pushing that opinion on Kim. I think it's important for young people to feel optimistic and confident about the future. They need to know the problems exist, but they also need to know there are a lot of good people who care and are working on solutions to them." I don't think Andy ever understood that it was his choice to look at the situation the way he did. Focusing on the negative was what made him feel our environmental plight was hopeless. When we focus on the solution rather than the problem, nothing seems hopeless.

In reality we are free to choose our own thoughts, but until we awaken to how thoughts influence our lives, we will not give much importance to disciplining our thinking. When we understand that good or bad is attracted into our lives by the pattern of our thoughts, choosing our thoughts and beliefs wisely becomes very important.

CHOOSING YOUR LIFE

How receptive to change are you? If we fear change, our beliefs will be rigid and our thoughts judgmental. We will be distrustful of anyone with ideas that are different from our own. Unless we are open to change we will not be able to free ourselves from outside influences; we will not be able to think independently. Being willing to change makes possible our ability to choose our own beliefs and become our own person.

Ask yourself the question, "What do I want in my life?" If we want peace, we must think thoughts of peace. Everyone says they want peace, but their thoughts are filled with everything but peace. Angry, aggressive thoughts will not bring a person peace. Can you think of someone you know who has an angry, aggressive nature? Are their lives peaceful or filled with unrest? If we want peace in our lives we must not allow fear to cause us to think hateful, harmful, savage, or cruel thoughts toward anyone.

If you want success in your life, you must focus on your strengths and not on your weaknesses. Disregard your weaknesses and keep on working toward your goal. See your goal as being true, and see it as though it already has been attained. This will help create the reality of it in your life. Don't let a few setbacks destroy your confidence. Be persistent and know the outcome you desire is real.

I was teaching sixth grade one year when I decided to try something different. At the beginning of a new grade period I announced my plan to the class. "As of right now, each of you in this class has an A in every subject."

My students didn't understand. No assignments had been made and no grades had been earned yet.

"What I'm saying is that I've started all of you off with an A in every subject." The class began to whisper among themselves. They were wondering if their teacher was losing it. "I just want everyone to know how it feels to have straight A's," I explained. "Right now, each of you is an A student, and it is up to you to keep it that way." I went on to show them what just one F would do to their A average. I promised that no matter how many of them chose to work hard and keep their A average, I would give A's to everyone who deserved them. At the end of that grade period, more students had averaged 90% or better in each subject than at any other time during my previous five years of teaching. It amazed even me. A simple change in the way these students looked at themselves gave them the motivation to work harder and achieve more than they ever had before. So think of yourself as an A student. Think of yourself as a success, and then follow up with the hard work necessary to make it so.

If we want harmony and great relationships in our lives, we must think thoughts of love, acceptance, and forgiveness. It is reasonable to expect respect if we have given respect. Other than this, it is best not to have expectations toward our loved ones. This was a difficult lesson for me to learn. As my mother got older, she phoned me less and less. She stopped sending birthday cards or gifts. She relied on me entirely to maintain our communication. This change in her behavior left me feeling hurt and angry. I felt that she should phone me sometimes, and that she should recognize her children's and grandchildren's birthdays. Finally, after many pain-filled months, I realized that the only way I could free myself from the pain I was feeling was to accept this change in her and drop my expectations. *Is my relationship with my mother going to depend on whether she phones or sends a card?* I asked myself. When I wasn't thinking of it emotionally, I knew that her age and health problems were the reasons behind her inattention. After some thoughtful self-examination, I admitted to myself that it was my insecurity and need for her approval that was causing my hurt. When I accepted this, I was able to let go of my expectations and love her unconditionally. The greatest gift we can give someone is to allow them to be themselves and live their lives as they choose.

If we want health in our lives, we must not focus on illness. Yes, there will be times when we don't feel well, but we must recognize that health is our natural state. Our body has a built-in system for keeping us healthy and for restoring us to perfect health when we're sick. We should not give encouragement to our illnesses by dwelling on them or looking for sympathy from others. If we recognize our good health each day and think of ourselves as being healthy, we find this to be true. I remember seeing an interview with a friend of Ryan White, the teenager who died from AIDS, in which the interviewer asked if they had talked much about his illness. "No," she said, "Ryan focused on living, not on dying." He'd had a positive outlook, even faced with his own mortality. The last months of his life were full, significant, and satisfying because he chose to make them that way.

If we want prosperity in our life, we must not focus on poverty. We must think of ourselves as having every-thing we need at the moment and stop ourselves from believing in lack, or in thinking that there isn't enough to go around. Many of us are taught to believe by our family or church that there is something noble in being poor, that money and greed are synonymous. "Money is the root of all evil" is a saying we've all heard. We choose whether or not to believe this, and our conviction may have a subconscious influence on how much money we allow ourselves to acquire.

It is difficult for us to understand that the source of

poverty is a state of mind. But many people who were born into meager surroundings never thought of themselves as being poor. Some people might say that Abraham Lincoln was born in poverty, but I don't think he thought that. If he had dwelled on the lack in his life, he never would have become our sixteenth president. I've heard many successful people, when speaking of their early years, say something to this effect: "We were poor but we didn't know it." The fact is, if you don't think you are poor, you aren't. Remember the story of my daughter not winning the thousand dollars when the radio station called her? She was terribly upset because she'd lost what to her seemed like a fortune.

"Are you any worse off now than you were before the phone call?" I asked.

"No . . ." she stammered, "but I could have bought so many neat clothes."

"Would the clothes have made you a better person?"

"Kids at school like you and want to be your friend if you dress cool."

I felt her pain as I remembered how it was in junior high. "I know it seems that way, but if they like you because of the clothes you wear, are they true friends?"

She frowned. I could see she was thinking it over. Changing our attitudes doesn't come easily, however, and after a few seconds she muttered, "I needed that money."

The truth was that she already had everything she really needed. A warm bed to sleep in at night, enough food to eat and clothes to wear, and a family who loved her. Still I understood how she felt. Our society has been assaulted with messages that more is better. Everyone is pushing and shoving, trying to get at the keyboard of our subconscious mind. Our only protection is the knowledge that they must go through us. We can accept or reject their message. We have the final say whether it gets programmed into our subconscious or not.

If we are thankful and feel genuine gratitude for all the good things in our lives, the good will increase. If our thoughts are filled with what we lack, if we feel slighted by life, if our general outlook is pessimistic and cynical, we will bring more of the same into our lives. So it is we who suffer when we do not monitor our thinking closely.

DISCIPLINED THOUGHT

Disciplined thought is conscious thought. When we become conscious of how our thoughts fill our lives—with either negative things such as pain, suffering, bad relationships, and poverty, or positive things such as peace, prosperity, love, and harmony—we will become aware of how important it is to master our thinking. We must take responsibility for our thoughts, and understand that we can control what we think. It takes work, however. After years of letting our thoughts control our lives, we find it takes determination and constant vigilance to achieve a disciplined mind.

Sometimes in the beginning stages of trying to control our thoughts, we experience obsessive thoughts that we seem powerless to control. Your parents have a huge fight and you are afraid they might get a divorce. You begin to imagine your mom talking to you about it. You begin having morose fantasies about the divorce and your unhappy life following it. You know these kinds of thoughts are destructive, so you try not to think them. The more you try to block them out, the more they seem to appear in your head. This is not disciplining your mind. It is repressing a fear, and fears must be dealt with. If you are torn up with doubt about your parents staying together, you need to talk with them and let them know how you're feeling. Whenever we repress our fears, we will have problems with obsessive thoughts. We need to confront our fears, examine them, and understand them.

Marilyn has a crush on a rock star. She thinks of him constantly. She doesn't get her homework or her chores done because she spends so much time daydreaming about him. Her desire for him is interfering with her education and her relationships with others. This situation is unhealthy and has become a destructive desire in her life. Marilyn must recognize how her thoughts are out of control and how they are hurting her. She must find healthy ways to satisfy the need that her fantasies are filling. She must focus her energy on something that will bring her true fulfillment.

Some things in our life we have no control over, but thinking is one thing we can control. No one can tell us what to think unless we allow them to. We must recognize that we are in charge of our thinking, and take charge. Positive thoughts surround us with positive energy that results in positive effects in our life. Our thoughts form a field of awareness that moves through and around us. This field is like a magnet that attracts to it only those things that reflect this awareness. If we want to attract good into our lives, we must think good thoughts. It follows the law of "Like produces like." Tigers produce tigers and cocker spaniels produce cocker spaniels. We attract to ourselves only that which we are. Knowing this puts the responsibility firmly on our own shoulders for creating the kind of life we want. If we have been raised in an atmosphere of anger and fear, if our parents are negative thinkers, then we will have to work extra hard to overcome the way of thinking we've grown accustomed to.

One way to do this is to use affirmations. These are positive statements declaring yourself as the person you want to be. If you want to be smart you might say, "I am intelligent, clever, knowledgeable, and wise." If you want to be popular you could say, "I am friendly, likable, confident, and open." Affirmations must always be stated in the present tense and said with enthusiasm and deep feeling. It is good to say affirmations just before going to sleep at night, the first thing when you wake up in the morning, and one time during the day. By saying these affirmative statements, you are programming a new perception of yourself into your subconscious mind. When you believe something subconsciously, it affects the way you perceive everything that happens. This is how your reality is created.

We must realize that we are unlimited spiritual beings with all the power and wisdom of God available to us, and that anything is possible. It is individuals who think positively and creatively who will find solutions to the many difficult problems in the world. Through us, world peace, harmony, and survival will be achieved.

CHAPTER VII

Spiritual Awareness

The first question I asked at the beginning of this book was, "Who are you?" I suggested that we are more than our bodies and more than the labels we've given ourselves. We must know who we are, apart from the obvious outer layer, in order to receive our inheritance as children of God, and to claim the good available to us.

Spiritual awareness is simply a complete and total awareness of who we are. You and I, all of us, are spiritual beings made in the image of God. This doesn't mean that we look like God or that God looks like a man or a woman. If you believe, as Jesus said, that God is spirit, then it is in spirit that we are alike. The spirit of God is infinite in intelligence, wisdom, truth, goodness, creativity, and unconditional love. I couldn't begin to describe all that God is because God is unlimited and . . . so are we! All that is in God is in us. But it is up to us to make the discovery. The only things that hold us back are our own mind and the illusions—the fantasies—that we've created about ourselves and our world.

Spiritual awareness begins with a willingness to exert the effort required to understand yourself. Examine your feelings, your fears, your anger, your value judgments, motivations, and beliefs, and question it all. This takes a lot of work and can sometimes be frightening, but the greatest love you can give yourself is this willingness to go through the flame of rebirth until you find out who you really are.

Unless we take the time to look at ourselves objectively, recognizing our feelings and finding where they are coming from, unless we can let go of our self-image long enough to see what's actually there, admitting how we really feel as opposed to how we think we should feel, we will not discover who we are. We will continue to hide from ourselves yet staunchly believe we know who we are.

If we want more out of life than mere survival, if we want a sense of fulfillment, a knowledge that our life is meaningful, then we need to awaken to ourselves as spiritual beings. We need to see beyond this lifetime and know that our spirit will survive the death of our bodies. Otherwise, we can easily succumb to despair. We must make the effort to discover our spiritual reality, or we will remain hidden from ourselves and never discover our true identity—the spiritual being that we are in truth. This true self lies deep within our subconscious. It could be described as the God within.

Many people throughout history have found God within themselves. Many of our great spiritual teachers have found God within and allowed that God spirit to direct and motivate their lives. Others have found the spirit that allows them to forget self, and to create, write, compose, speak, heal, etc. It is only by standing aside and letting the spirit work through me that I am able to write this book. Each day before I start to write, I spend time in meditation. Meditation helps me to let the inner wisdom that comes from God emerge in my writing. It also helps my subconscious release many of the things I've learned and the experiences that I've had that are significant for the book. You, too, can find this same

spirit and discover yourself as a spiritual being with unlimited potential.

When I began to spend thirty minutes a day in meditation my life improved in many ways. I began to feel
more in charge of my life. I was able to solve problems
more easily. I had more energy and my health improved. After a while I began to notice an inner strength
that I'd never had before. I was able to deal with difficult situations calmly and with confidence. Meditation
has benefited every area of my life.

Experiments prove that meditation relieves anxiety,
improves concentration, and releases creativity. Many
teachers believe it increases learning ability. The relax-
ation that comes from meditation allows the immune
system to work better. Meditation is a way of reaching
the spiritual part of you that is eternal. Think of a day
when everything has gone wrong at school. Friendship
problems or problems with teachers leave you uptight,
stressed, completely worn out. Meditation is a way of
letting it all go, recharging your energies, and enabling
yourself to face your problems and find solutions for
them. Emptying your mind of all thought and concern
slowly builds a spiritual reservoir that provides insight,
strength, persistence, and effectiveness in times of
trouble.

WHY SEEK SPIRITUAL AWARENESS?

Life can be difficult. It can be filled with pain, suffering,
unhappiness, and despair. But it can also be loving and
wonderful. Through the hard work of self-examination
and through a process of learning to let go of all the
things that are causing us such pain, we can find joy and
fulfillment.

We humans consist of three things: body, mind, and spirit. We spend endless hours caring for our bodies, exercising, eating right, caring for our teeth, hair, and skin, and spending huge amounts of money in the process. We spend time, too, improving our minds. We fill them with facts and figures, with huge amounts of information. But we spend practically no time caring for our spirit. We don't try to nurture it; often we're not even aware of it. If the way we care for our spiritual side were compared to our physical side, it would be like never brushing our teeth. Think of what would happen. Neglect causes pain and loss, and this is true whether we are talking about teeth or our spiritual nature.

When I was a teenager, I used to wonder what the most important thing in life was. I wondered if it was religion, or politics, or friendships, or education. Today a teenager could add many pressing concerns to that list—the environment, crime, drugs, injustice, prejudice. All of these things are important, but I have discovered that the most important thing of all is what goes on inside us. It doesn't matter what we devote our lives to, as much as what we become on the inside. It is sobering to realize that when we die all that we will take with us is the person we've become deep within. Our body dies. Our mind dies, along with all the knowledge we've accumulated with it. But the spirit lives on, and our spirit is all that we are in our heart. If we are filled with hate, regret, anger, and fear, this will be in our consciousness after our soul leaves our bodies. This is the real Hell. Hell isn't a place, it's a state of consciousness. Likewise, if, when we die, we are full of love, compassion, peace, and goodwill, this state of consciousness will be like Heaven, and we will be satisfied that our lives were well spent.

A person who is seeking spiritual awareness is offering himself a gift. The gift comes from the love that a person has for himself, and it will bring him joy, fulfillment, satisfaction, and peace. To be aware of our spiritual side is to be awake to the things in our heart. To be willing to grow spiritually is to be willing to awaken to life as it is. It's a willingness to see the log in our own eye rather than worrying about the speck in the eye of another. It's a willingness to drop judgment, pride, prejudice, and our beliefs. Now we can look at everything with a new openness and a new consciousness. This willingness to grow is the same thing as love.

What is the purpose of life, anyway? Why are we here? Some of us think we're here to make a name for ourselves, to accomplish great things, to accumulate wealth, possessions, prestige, and power. Others, certainly the great creative minds, have had a dedication above and beyond their own egos in the composition of great music, dance, poetry, and art. But most of us, in order to gauge the importance of what we think we are here for, should consider for a moment the questions we will ask ourselves on our death bed. Will your possessions really matter at that moment? Will your prestige or your power matter? When I visualize that moment, I see myself asking, "Has my life been well spent? Have I fulfilled my dreams?" and, most importantly, "Have I loved well?" Because all that really matters is love. The answers we have for these questions determine whether we leave this life in peace or not.

What Holds Us Back

It's hard to believe, but the biggest obstacle to spiritual growth, and the source of all other obstacles to it, is laziness. Everyone, child and adult alike, is lazy to some extent. Since love is helping oneself or another, through struggle, effort, and hard work, to achieve spiritual growth, it follows that nonlove, or the opposite of love, is an unwillingness to exert this effort, or laziness. Many of us refuse to grow spiritually because of the effort involved. Also, we want an immediate reward for our efforts. If we can't see something tangible, something we can point to like a new car or a slim new figure, we don't want to work for it. The rewards of spiritual growth are much more subtle. However, with the will to grow and a great deal of discipline, a strength of spirit evolves quietly, almost unnoticed, until one day we fully awaken to the truth of who we are.

One of the big things that keeps us from growing spiritually is fear. We are afraid of change. A new idea that threatens our view of life is scary and so we reject it immediately. Everyone is looking for security, and anything that might strip us of security is frightening. However, unless we are willing to risk our security and our beliefs about life, we cannot progress spiritually. We must let go of fear—fear of failure, fear of change, and the fear of revealing our true selves. If we never risk anything, we'll never do anything. Only through risk can we learn, grow, feel, and love. If we let ourselves be controlled by fear, we can never be free.

Another thing that will squelch the possibility for spiritual growth is cruelty. Cruelty is born out of fear and a desperate need to be in control. The boy who seems to derive pleasure from torturing cats, the girl who likes to intimidate classmates with threats and hateful remarks, the husband who beats his wife and children, are all suffering spiritually. Everyone is capable of cruelty. The difference between people who are cruel and people who are not is a person's capacity for empathy. Empathy is the ability to put yourself in another's place and feel as they would feel. Empathy comes from a deep sensitivity to others, be they people or animals. A person's capacity for empathy comes from his background and his willingness to set his own feelings aside for a moment and feel what another would feel. Every action we take has an equal reaction. Our cruelty injures our spirit and is a setback on our journey to spiritual enlightenment.

Blaming others is one of the most harmful things for spiritual growth. It can even lead to mental illness. Blaming another is destructive to our relationship with them, and we risk severing that relationship when we insist on affixing blame. We must accept total responsibility for ourselves if we are to be mentally and spiritually healthy. As long as we blame our parents, our poverty, our peers, or anything else for the things that have gone wrong in our lives, we will not be able to possess our own lives. When we blame others we make ourselves victims. As long as you view yourself as a victim, you cannot inherit your birthright, as a child of God, to happiness, abundance, fulfillment, and unlimited possibilities.

Our rigidity holds us back from growing spiritually. As we get older we become extremely attached to our beliefs. These beliefs, which we've accepted from parents, ministers, teachers, and others, are simply opinions from others that we've chosen to make our own. These beliefs offer us security, so we hold fast to them and defend them with all our might. Even though at times our beliefs cause us great pain and set upon us great burdens, we still hold on to them with tenacity and a rigid inflexibility that freezes our progress on the spiritual path.

We think we know what's right and wrong, and we are unwilling to consider anything that clashes with our belief. Our sense of right and wrong develops into a passion motivated entirely by emotion. For example, Jim and Theresa feel deeply that abortion is wrong and their passion on this issue compels them to do anything that it takes to force their belief (opinion) on others. Behind their passion is a self-righteous attitude that says they are right and anyone who disagrees with them is wrong. People like Jim and Theresa, who let passion and emotion rule their lives, will never be open to change.

Religion is supposed to offer us comfort, but in many cases it does the opposite. When Mary Ann's brother, Shawn, died, the fact that he had been an agnostic caused her great pain. She loved her brother. He had been a caring, loving individual who had always been there for her, but, as a devout Christian, she had been taught that any person who had not accepted Jesus Christ as his savior would not go to Heaven. The thought of Shawn burning in Hell caused Mary Ann great torment and placed an enormous burden on her. Mary Ann's religious beliefs prevented her from letting go of her fears and trusting that Shawn was in the hands of a caring God who loves us unconditionally. When we recognize that what a person is in his heart is more important than what he says he believes, we will be moving toward spiritual enlightenment. And when we know God as unconditional love we will be comforted.

The concept of sin as being destructive to our soul and a sure ticket to Hell causes great pain and can even result in mental illness. A healthier way to look at what has traditionally been labeled as sin is to consider it a mistake. Everyone makes mistakes. We can learn from our mistakes if we admit them and make the connection between the mistake and the result of it. We can learn to liberate ourselves from the urgings of those who want us to feel guilty for our sins. Guilt blocks our understanding. By refusing to wallow in guilt and choosing instead to use love and compassion to understand the ignorance that has caused us to "sin," we can awaken to the lesson of our mistake and be healed. In this way our spirit evolves to a level where we no longer make that mistake.

Religious dogma has too often caused our harsh judgments toward ourselves and others. We can release ourselves from our judgments by seeing mistakes as opportunities for growth and refusing to condemn ourselves or others. In this way we free ourselves from unnecessary pain and suffering. In order to proceed on the spiritual path we must be willing to open ourselves to new possibilities. We must be willing to let go of our old beliefs and become open—not by trading our old beliefs for new ones, but by being forever flexible. We need to constantly broaden our view of life and see more than our limited experience can show us. If God meant for our experience alone to lead us to truth, He would have given us all the same experience. I don't have to experience prejudice directly to know it's wrong. By using empathy I can vicariously feel the pain of prejudice. By imagining myself to be a victim of prejudice I awaken to a truth that my direct experience might possibly never teach me.

Our experiences are different, but all of us have our share of good and bad times. Our will determines how we react to them. It is human nature to welcome the good with joy and gratitude, and to resist the bad. We try to prevent bad things from happening, but the fact is, no matter how careful and conscientious we are, they are part of life. As long as we resist what has happened, our thoughts and feelings will be agitated and in turmoil. The only way to bring peace back into our lives is to accept the bad as a natural part of living. Then, if we are receptive, we may discover a new revelation of truth that the bad experience has shown us.

Brenda was a cheerleader at the local high school. She was popular, pretty, and seemed to have everything. Her main interests were boys, makeup, clothes, and hair styles. Then Brenda was in an automobile crash. Her face was scarred, and she was paralyzed from the waist down. At the time, the accident was a horrible disaster in Brenda's life. Now, several years later, Brenda is supporting herself by creating extraordinary oil paintings. "The accident changed me," she said to a group of teenagers, "but only for the better. Before, I was superficial . . . silly even. I didn't care deeply about anything. All I wanted from life was to have a blast. After the accident I spent several months depressed. I just closed down emotionally. I wanted to die. Then one morning after I'd returned home from the hospital, I noticed an enormous white owl sitting on the fence outside my window. I watched as he sat motionless for a long while, his white feathers puffed out. Finally he stretched his huge wings and soared to some high branches of the eucalyptus tree in our yard." Brenda hesitated, then with great clarity she continued. "Somehow I saw myself in that owl. I recognized that I had a choice. I could continue to sit in my room, detached from life and emotionless, or I could spread my wings and fly. I knew I could enjoy life again, that my life could be meaningful. And, you know, life is so much more than I'd ever imagined it could be."

Brenda discovered a depth of spirit she didn't know

she had. She was ready to receive from her experience insight, wisdom, and a new awareness that revealed to her the wonders and miracles that life has to offer. She soon found she had a creative talent with paints and paintbrush that both surprised and pleased her. She had come to the point where she felt genuinely grateful for her new life.

How We Achieve Spiritual Awareness

Spiritual growth involves freeing ourselves from preconceived ideas about the world and humanity, and constantly revising these ideas as we understand and accept new knowledge. We must be willing to let go of our old beliefs and allow ourselves to see the truth, even when that truth conflicts with how we have always thought. We must be willing to open our minds to all possibilities and to stop ourselves from rejecting an idea because it makes us uncomfortable. We must question everything. Through questioning, seeking, doubting, experiencing, and keeping open, we will discover our own truth. This truth will have validity. It will be entirely personal and genuinely our own.

Hoping, wishing, or believing does not lead to spiritual awareness. Only experience and inner reflection can carry us along this path. To seek truth, to challenge yourself and question, to be willing to change your ideas and beliefs, to risk your old self and finally to let it go for a new self is to grow spiritually. We are spiritual beings with the potential of great awareness, but without self-examination and the willingness to let go of old notions and prejudices we cannot discover our spirituality.

So it is in the letting go that we discover our spirituality. Life teaches us this. First we must let go of our childhood and the days of no responsibility and utter self-centeredness. As we get older, life will teach us to let go of people we love, places we've lived, and possessions we've grown attached to. We must also learn to let go of the things our mind has accepted. When we hold on with a deathlike grip to our beliefs, our ideas of right and wrong, our pride, judgments, and fears, it is our spirit that is being strangled. Life is a harsh teacher, and holding on too long will eventually cause anger and resentment to fill our hearts. A black cloud of sorrow and unhappiness will follow us throughout our days. The man who refuses to speak to his daughter because she married outside the faith, the rich woman who refuses to give to the needy because she is insecure and filled with fear, the teenager whose pride drives him to mock another so that he'll look good in front of his friends—all are driven by the mind's destructive illusions of how life is. It is only by letting go that these people can find their spirituality. If we do not let go willingly, and if we always define who we are in terms of the physical and of what our mind accepts as true, we will suffer greatly when life harshly strips us of these things. If we have ignored the spiritual part of us and refused to listen to our heart, these losses will slash and mutilate whatever is left of us. But if we have learned, along the way, to surrender gracefully those things that our ego has identified as "us," then we will find the real person that lies beneath our self-created image—the self that is eternal and that will be with us always.

The longer we resist letting go of our old selves, the longer we delay our awakening. We must learn to live in the now, being totally aware of each moment as a precious gift but having the courage to let go when life says it's time. We must have faith that in letting go and allowing ourselves to become open we will be filled with the spiritual awareness that was there all along but that was buried beneath our own ego. By the willingness to let go, we transcend our ego—we go beyond ego to discover who we really are. This discovery, like any great discovery, takes work, perseverance, commitment, and, above all else, love.

I urge you to continue a quest for your own spirituality. Life is a process of experiencing, learning, and growing in awareness and understanding of who and what you are. As you enter into your adult life, seek out opportunities to increase that awareness. Take time to commune with God. Submit yourself to His guidance and let love be the motivating force behind everything you think, say, and do for the rest of your life.

AWAKENING

Choose your thoughts wisely,
Be motivated by love,
Know you are spirit,
Perfect and divine.

God is within you,
He speaks to your heart,
Be silent and know Him,
Infinite Truth.

With clear understanding,
With wisdom and grace,
Spirit awakens,
Mind evolves.

Recommended Reading

Harold Bloomfield, *Making Peace with Your Parents* (New York: Random House, 1983). Shows how to establish a loving, fulfilling relationship with parents, even difficult ones.

Alan Cohen, *Dare to Be Yourself* (Somerset, N.J.: Alan Cohen Publications, 1991). Helps strip away the masks we've hidden behind so we can live life joyfully, genuinely, and powerfully.

Alan Loy McGinnis, *The Friendship Factor* (Minneapolis: Augsburg Publishing House, 1979). Shares the secrets of close, healthy friendships.

David McNally, *Even Eagles Need a Push* (Eden Prairie, Minn.: Transform Press, 1990). A motivational book for young people who are deciding what to do with their lives.

M. Scott Peck, *The Road Less Traveled* (New York: Simon and Schuster, 1978). Offers a deep insight into love, self-discipline, and one's own spiritual journey.

Paul Wilson, *The Calm Technique* (New York: Bantam Books, 1989). A simple, clear guide to meditation.

Acknowledgments

I wish to extend sincere gratitude to those spiritual teachers who have helped me achieve openness, insight, and my own spiritual awareness. I am deeply thankful for their classes, discourses, and books that have helped me discover my own path. Through their loving contributions I've found self-confidence, a better way to think, and the key to happiness.

I wish to thank my daughters, Kim, Krista, Beth, and Sarah, and also Jeff Welch, for their suggestions and proofreading. A big thank-you to Ken Wagoner and Mike Floyd for their computer expertise.

I especially want to thank M. Scott Peck, Kathleen Fitzpatrick, Fred Hills, and Daphne Bien for their thoughts, advice, support, and assistance. I sincerely appreciate the faith they have shown in my work.